JESUS,
THE SALESMAN

JESUS, THE SALESMAN

How to Use the Awesome Power of Persuasion

R. W. KLAMM

iUniverse, Inc.
Bloomington

Jesus, The Salesman
How to Use the Awesome Power of Persuasion

iUniverse books may be ordered through booksellers or by contacting:

iUniverse
1663 Liberty Drive
Bloomington, IN 47403
www.iuniverse.com
1-800-Authors (1-800-288-4677)

Because of the dynamic nature of the Internet, any web addresses or links contained in this book may have changed since publication and may no longer be valid. The views expressed in this work are solely those of the author and do not necessarily reflect the views of the publisher, and the publisher hereby disclaims any responsibility for them.

Any people depicted in stock imagery provided by Thinkstock are models, and such images are being used for illustrative purposes only.
Certain stock imagery © Thinkstock.

ISBN: 978-1-4759-5981-9 (sc)
ISBN: 978-1-4759-5982-6 (ebk)

Library of Congress Control Number: 2012920999

Printed in the United States of America

iUniverse rev. date: 11/10/2012

CONTENTS

PREFACE.. ix

Chapter 1.   SALESMAN SUPREME 1
Chapter 2.   ASSUMING THE DESIRED RESULT 5
Chapter 3.   THE SECRET IDENTITY................................ 11
Chapter 4.   THE CHOICE: SIMPLE and WEIGHTED........ 17
Chapter 5.   SPECIAL INCENTIVE.................................... 23
Chapter 6.   FEAR OF LOSS.. 27
Chapter 7.   THE RULE OF PHYSICAL ACTION 31
Chapter 8.   REQUEST FOR ACTION 35
Chapter 9.   QUICK-FIX SHORT CUTS............................. 39

ABOUT THE AUTHOR... 45
APPENDIX 47

To those who inspired this book:

Rev. Walter L Brown Jr., who helped me understand God as a personal reality rather than a mere idea.

William C. Standart and John B O'Hern, who have shown me that those outstanding advertising men do not need to sacrifice their Christian principles in the market place.

Cover idea and illustrations by Athena Stringfellow

PREFACE

The essence of democracy is compromise and agreeable disagreement. Unfortunately, today the disagreement has become disagreeable in itself, and compromise has become a dirty word. My background forces me to cry out in protest.

As a long-standing Presbyterian and Methodist, I have been steeped in the principals of charity and good will. As a member of the Fellowship of Christian Magicians, I have prepared numerous persuasions for Gospel performers.

When I became involved in the hard sell world of advertising, I had to deal with the sharp contrast of selling to make a quick buck. The over riding edict was sell, sell, sell, regardless of the ethics. I was quickly disillusioned.

One day my boss brought me a book, which described the various methods of persuasion, and asked me to summarize and simplify the descriptions for a seminar he was conducting.

As I worked, I began to realize that it was not the principles of advertising, but the people involved, that were the problem. Truth is truth wherever you find it, and people will be people no matter whom or where they may be. They can be selfish, greedy, lazy, angry, antagonistic, ignorant, and stupid. It is the course of least resistance.

When I actually began to study the tenants of advertising, I discovered that those principles were no different than the principles I was explaining to my Sunday school class of fifth graders. The principles governing the divisive world of advertising were the same as those espoused by none less than Jesus of Nazareth. There is detailed evidence to that fact in the Bible.

Our failure to recognize this is tearing our world apart. Instead of working together in cooperation, compromise, and agreeable disagreement, we have become polarized, one against the other. We have become right fighters. Each of us has decided that we are right, and any who disagree are absolutely wrong. It is man against wife; child against parent and visa versa; Republican against Democrat; business against labor, corporations gobbling up each other, black against white is kept in check, but just barely. Even religions are often pitted vehemently against each other.

In each of these struggles there must be a winner, and for each winner there is at least one angry loser. We have become a society of winners and losers instead of friends and neighbors. Instead of gaining strength from our differences, we have violated each other because of them.

This book attempts to bridge some of those gaps. It is divided into two quite unequal sections. The first section deals with various methods of persuasion. It includes chapters two through eight. The second section is a long chapter nine, labeled *Quick and Easy Shortcuts*. Knowing that people gravitate to short cuts, I recommend that you read this book, in front to back order first. When it comes to putting these thoughts to work in your life, start with chapter nine. Then go back and refer to other chapters as needed.

1

SALESMAN SUPREME

Down through the ages, Jesus has been named many things by many people; but rarely, if ever, has he been called a "salesman." For some, the label may even seem to be sacrilegious. No wonder! These days, our major exposure to salesmen is via the blaring sales pitch on the media, and includes hucksters and cheats of all types. Each one will tell you that his product is better than all the rest, whether it is the truth or not. His main center of interest is not you, but himself and making the sale. It is understandable to a degree. Today, the competition is tough, and like everyone else, he needs to make a living. But where is the limit? Watering down ingredients to make a bigger profit, or merely packaging a product in a new wrapper, and then calling it "improved" is way over the line.

A real salesman has the customer's needs at heart, not strictly his own. He is kind, considerate, tells the truth, possibly because he only wants our repeat business, but also he sincerely wants to help us. It is for our best interests that he wants us to change to what he is offering. In Biblical terms, he wants us to *repent* to something better.

Jesus was that kind of salesman. In fact, he might easily be called the greatest salesman the world has ever known. His persuasions were so powerful that the authorities began to feel threatened by His message, and killed him. Nevertheless, he brought world changes that have lasted down through the ages.

By contrast, back in that era, there was another salesman, who was more like our current hucksters and pitchmen. He carried the same basic message as Jesus, but he ranted and raved, scolded and

1

blamed, and finally lost his head completely over the matter. I refer here to John the Baptist.

The differences in techniques between the two are worlds apart; and that makes all the difference in how effective the messages were.

That is what this book is all about. I—

Pardon me, but does this chapter begin to sound more like an introduction than a chapter? I guess that's because it sort of is that. A lot of people do not read introductions to books. I thought this was a "must read" before you began, so I made it into a chapter. Hope you do not feel manipulated.

Now as I was about to say, there are powerful tools of persuasion that are easy to use and easily available, but we fail to use them. We fail because most people don't know what they are, how they work, think they know better, consider them dishonest, or believe that the product will speak for itself. For these reasons, I call these persuasive techniques "secret." Very few people know very little about them.

We will take each, one at a time, define each; explain the way each works separately and in combination; provide examples from the Bible, media, and real life. We will also show how gospel clowns, ventriloquists, puppeteers, magicians, and the like can use them in performance.

With such a wide variety of examples, it is my hope that these techniques will become a permanent part of you and your relationship with others . . . but only if you want that to happen.

Before we get into the business of each individual method, you should become aware that there is a framework known to most speakers, writers, and various communicators, on which to hang their basic message. The letters AIDA represent that framework. Every persuasion touches on these points. They represent the words *attention, interest, desire,* and *action.*

Using this book as an example to demonstrate, the title and cover design is there to grab your *attention.* The sub-title tells you a little more to create *interest. Desire* is the critical part of the persuasion. The back cover copy is designed to stimulate *desire. Action* urges you on to do what is specifically needed. Jesus frequently charged his audiences with, "Go, and sin no more."

There is yet one more secret I need to reveal. When it comes to *desire*, we are not logical creatures. We choose on the basis of our emotions, rather than our logic. We don't like to think of ourselves as being that way, but that's the way we are built. It is easy for us to be led down the wrong path, if we are unaware.

Knowing how these techniques work may protect you from their unscrupulous use. It may also help you to guide family members and others to more productive choices, without being overbearing. In the right hands, these methods can work miracles!

2

ASSUMING THE DESIRED RESULT

What did you expect?

This is, by far, the most important of all of the persuasive principles, and undoubtedly the point at which to begin. Set this technique into motion even before you decide what you want to say. It will help you select other persuasive techniques, and unconsciously affect the choice of every word you say. It is also an extremely powerful sales technique, in and of itself.

Before you ever begin, assume that your listener already accepts and wants whatever you want for him. In other words, assume the best of your listener. Believe it deep down in your heart and soul, and you will make it come to pass.

I know, I know! This sounds like the same meaningless nonsense pushed by so many motivational books, but this is different. It is not to be mistaken for mere wishful thinking, or an attempt to build your confidence. It is a direct action you need to take to get others to want to do what you want them to do. Be careful here. It must not be your purpose or privilege to force them or browbeat them into your way of thinking. You must let them discover their own ways for themselves. Your mode of thinking should be to believe, not to convince.

Teachers tell us that children will act pretty much the way we expect them to act. Actors know that if they believe the part they are playing, so will their audience believe. Psychologists tell us that everyone wants to do the right thing. It's just that sometimes people get confused, and make poor choices.

If you truly assume the best of those you would influence, and really believe they will make the very best decisions for themselves, if only they knew what you had available to share, then you may be of some real help to your audience, and to yourself as well.

Christ said, "As a man thinketh, so is he."

In other words, you directly affect the results by the attitude you bring to the situation. Parents, teachers, Christian communicators, all of us are starting off on the wrong foot, when we point a finger and accuse, scold, and shame. By doing so, we actually tend to encourage bad behavior. That's right. We encourage bad behavior by preaching against it.

So what in the world can we do about changing things? Are we just supposed to fold our hands and let the world roll over us? No indeed, but we can think with a different attitude.

Let's take a closer look at how this technique works. Suppose someone with tickets to a road show approaches us.

He says, "You don't want to buy any tickets, do you?"

We say, "Of course not." If he doesn't think so, we will agree. After all, he knows more about it than we do.

Now, let's suppose that, instead, he says. "Do you want to buy some tickets?"

That's more positive, but still pretty neutral. We are inclined to shrug our shoulders and say, "I doubt it."

Just then, another salesman rounds the corner with similar tickets. He says, "Boy am I glad I found you. I've been saving these two tickets for you. The minute I heard about this particular show, I knew you'd be interested."

We think to ourselves, "Maybe we ought to be interested. He seems so sure. Does he know something that we don't know?"

Now, let us look at a more complicated Biblical example: John 8: 3-11 (KJV)

This is the incident where some of the men-folk of the town are about to stone a woman to death for having sex with one (or maybe even more than one) of these guys. It's undoubtedly a small town. Everyone knows everyone else's business. Maybe some male rivalries are in play. A jealous wife or two may be in the background, urging things on.

Somehow Jesus gets caught in the middle. The crowd is out for blood. Instead of taking sides or arguing them down, Jesus avoids any confrontational eye contact by studying the ground.

"Let him who is without sin throw the first stone," he says.

Is there anyone then or now who meets that qualification? Is there no one who will add a lie to his other transgressions by throwing the first stone? Certainly there is no one here, in front of friends and neighbors who will do so.

Jesus assumes that they do not want to be caught openly in a lie. He assumes the best of them, and they do not want to destroy that

7

image. He also assumes the best of the woman when he says, "Go and sin no more."

He knows that she will not be able to make a complete turn about, but will try to do better. She will do her best to live up to his expectations.

Jesus' entire life was a continual example of assuming the best of people. That's the way it was from Pilate to Judas, and including the sly ones all along the way who tried to entrap him.

For our performance example, we have two. They both involve audience volunteers. A performer must be careful never to make a volunteer look foolish. He represents the entire audience. Whatever you do to one, you do to the other. If you make your volunteer look like a fool, your audience will hurt for him and resent you, no matter how funny it may play. A couple of examples are in order here.

The first one happened when I was watching a show at a magic convention. The magician asked for a lady volunteer. The lady next to me raised her hand. I sensed what was coming, and almost stopped her, but was too late. I consoled myself that it was a magic convention. She was likely a magician's wife, and probably knew what she was doing.

The trick involved tying two handkerchiefs together and making a third one magically appear, tied in between the first two. To make this happen, the lady is asked to tuck the first knot into her bosom, but instead of a third hanky appearing there, a bra is found, instead.

When it happened, I was surprised at her reactions. I guess I was wrong in my concerns. She was a good sport and seemed to be having a great time. The biggest surprise came when she returned to her seat.

She leaned over and whispered in my ear. "I didn't know that was going to happen. I'll never agree to be a magician's volunteer again"

Later, another audience member stopped me and said, "I was so embarrassed for her."

Another trick that makes for a good example of what to avoid, is called The Tricky Turvy Bottles. It is a set of two bottles, each with its own covering tube. The magician and his young volunteer each take a set, bottles inside the tubes, and turn them this way and that. The kid always ends up with his bottle the wrong way, and everyone laughing at him. Bad!

How much better it would be if the performer were the one who always ends up wrong? He could then build up the amazing skill of his marvelous assistant. By building up his assistant, he endears himself to the entire audience.

Using this technique as a base, a good salesman can add other techniques to increase the power of his influence.

3

THE SECRET IDENTITY

Who? Me?

Here is a technique which everyone, and especially performers will recognize. In its non-sales mode, it is simply a story. Magicians will recognize it as a patter story, clowns as the comedy sketch, vents (ventriloquists) as dialogue, and puppeteers as the story line or plot. Even print and other advertising media frequently include a short skit. Properly directed and fully developed, it can be very powerful. This technique is called "*The Secret Identity.*"

In this method, a story is told in which a character has a problem. Either the character or the problem or both are ones with which the audience can easily identify. A solution to the problem is then presented. The solution just happens to include the action you want your audience to take.

If the audience identifies in a positive way with the story character, he will tend to adopt the solution chosen by the character. If he identifies negatively with the character, he will choose to go exactly the opposite direction.

It is important to the listener's ego that he be allowed to decide this identity on his own, secretly. If he senses in any way that you believe the story is about him, he will resent it.

Secrecy is especially important if the identification is negative. He must always be free to deny that he was ever the kind of distasteful character your story may depict—even though he secretly knows that he is. Allowing your listener to make his own identification also means he will hold to the solution longer, because it belongs to him, personally.

To make it easy for your listeners to identify, select basic human traits for your central character. Use traits such as hate, fear, yearnings, greed, love, warmth of spirit, and the like. These may be exaggerated and distorted for the sake of humor. The important thing is that they realistically fit the situation, so that though your listeners may laugh, they may secretly see themselves.

Then present your solution. Here, it is absolutely crucial that the movement into the solution be logical and natural. The solution must also be specific. Once the listener accepts it, he must know how he can put it to work in his own life.

The media is full of such examples. Unfortunately, there are more examples that are bad than good. Nevertheless, we can learn much by studying both. First, here is an example that is all wrong. We see a woman holding her head in pain. In a most unattractive way, she lashes out in anger at her noisy children. Then we hear a voice say, "Don't take your headache out on your children. If you love them, use XYZ product."

Note that it is specifically *your* headache and *your* children. The identification is made positively with a negative character and sales dropped drastically. It was soon discovered that even many old customers were dropping the product. It didn't take the advertiser long to get the message and dropped the commercial.

Here is a more effective use of the technique. A man sits on the edge of the bed with his hand to his stomach. In one line he mutters the entire story. "I can't believe I ate the whole thing."

Though we are not identified directly, we can see ourselves. We instantly see and laugh at our own foolishness and take heed. We have made a positive identification with a very unpleasant situation, and we have made the identification ourselves. His solution will be our solution. Whatever he decides will be just fine for us, too. Years later, the advertiser is still using this approach.

For our Biblical example, please turn to Luke 10: 25-37 (KJV). This parable of the Good Samaritan is a masterful stroke in the use of both positive and negative identification. The listener has a choice of identities from which to select. If he identifies with the Samaritan, the natural result is to adopt that course of action as his own.

If he finds he is one of the bad guys, Jesus leaves the door open for him to secretly slip over to the proper side. The bad guys are defined in terms of a general category, so it is easier to change course and deny ever being a part of that group.

Ventriloquists will find this method easy to use. If the dummy is really dumb, it sets up a negative identification. The audience can join with the vent in correcting the dummy, for doing things that they know they do themselves. Thus, your audience begins to become self-correcting.

What a wonderful technique for parents to use when reading a story to their young children. You can encourage them to tell the story character how he should behave. It is only when the dummy is somehow made into a hero for all his shenanigans that the kids want to imitate him.

Here is an example of this technique used in a story for the performer. The story is designed to go with making a paper tree. Making the paper tree provides the visual while the performer is telling the story.

THE GIANT LITTLE CHRISTMAS TREE

Once there was a great, grand and glorious evergreen tree which grew deep in the forest. For many long years it stood there, growing straight and tall and proud. The North Wind was its friend. It whispered often through its branches and the tree would whisper back.

"Some day I will be the grandest tree of all. Then the people of the town will decorate me with all sorts of bright glittering balls, and I will display my glory in honor of the Christ Child."

One day, some men did come. Their eyes grew wide when they saw the great tree.

"This tree is the most valuable in the entire forest," he heard them say, and his branches creaked with pride.

But instead of taking him to the town square, the men carried him up to the paper mill at the edge of town. There he was chopped and pounded and rolled and pressed into paper.

"How can this be when I have done everything right," the tree groaned. "Is there no God? To think that I should become nothing but common paper."

And so it was that the great tree found his way as an old newspaper, to a shabby room in a sad and forgotten part of town. But then he heard his friend, the North Wind, rattle under the loose fitting door.

"Life does not always give us what we expect, but God gives us the strength to endure. Your life has been grander than you can imagine. Your branches have given shelter to birds. Your wood has provided work to men in the mill, and pages for many books. Now in this shabby room, you have at last been given a chance to satisfy your lifelong dream."

There in a forgotten corner lay a small child, sick, weak, and forlorn. Then it was that the tree began to realize that God sometimes has a plan of his own for our lives. Quickly, with the help of the old North Wind, he rolled himself up into a tube.

"Greatest is not always grandest."

"Then he transformed himself into the only real Christmas the sick child would have—a little Christmas tree with a giant heart.

Method: (Ordinarily we would not provide specific details like this on construction or workings of props. It is not considered good etiquette among magicians to share trade secrets with the public, nor is it truly within the scope of this book. We will include them only when the particular explanation is of general knowledge, or necessary to a better understanding of the persuasive technique involved.)

Use three or four full-size sheets of newspaper, opened out flat. Roll a paper tube, using one sheet at a time, over lapping them end to end, as you go. The tube should be a little less than 2 inches in diameter. Where the edges meet, overlap them by about four inches. This may be done before the program or even while telling the story.

Place a rubber band around the tube, about four inches from one end.

When ready to actually make the tree, begin at the end opposite the rubber band. Make three or four tears running lengthwise along the tube. These tears should be evenly spaced around the tube and stop a little past the center. To produce the tree, pull up on the inside of the tube. The torn strips will become the branches.

4

THE CHOICE:
SIMPLE AND WEIGHTED

Eeny Meeny, the choice is minor

This technique is one that is so easy to understand and use, that you may have already figured it out from the chapter title. Here is how it works:

Ask your listener to make a choice. On the surface the choice appears to be relatively unimportant, but either way he chooses, the choice leads him one step closer to what you want him to do. For example, "Do you like the red balloon or the blue one best?"

Either way the listener answers, he has indicated an interest toward the balloon. Of course, he could refuse to commit, or come up with an answer in a different direction, but that takes thought. He has not actually been asked to purchase the balloon, so he feels safe to answer. Still, he has moved one step closer to a purchase of the balloon.

The next step would move us to a technique we will discuss in chapter seven. It would require handing him a balloon with a string attached, and commenting, "Here, would you like to hold it?"

We are bombarded by a myriad of such choices each day, all of them trying to get us to buy, buy, buy:

"Do you like the silk or cotton better?"

"Would you prefer the large economy size? You get half again as much for only fifteen cents more."

"Pick any flavor you want."

Many parents may have discovered, on their own, how effective this offering of choices can be:

"Do you want to lie on the floor or the bed when I put your diaper on?" This bypasses any argument over whether or not the child wants the diaper changed.

"Do you want to do what I ask, or do you want to stand in the corner?"

I break into a particularly broad smile when my daughter-in-law says to one of her children, "Do you want to do what I say, or do you want to stand in the corner, and then do what I say?"

It does not matter which way your listener decides. Either way he chooses, he moves in the direction of the desired result.

In all of these last three instances, all of the choices except the last one are *Simple Choices*. The last one is a *Weighted Choice*. It is set up from the beginning to offer one choice as the more desirable. In either method, the listener does have a choice, but either choice leads to what you want to accomplish.

Here is another example using both. Suppose you are considering the purchase of a new vacuum cleaner. The salesman starts by giving you a few simple choices.

"Do you prefer the standard or deluxe model?"

Either way you answer, you have committed yourself to consider his vacuum cleaner over some other brand.

There may be a few more choices along the way like, "May I use your phone to see if we have that model in stock?" or "Will this be cash or charge?" These *Simple Choices* are all it takes to make you feel obligated and nudge the sale in your direction.

As to the *Weighted Choice*, the standard approach is to clean a spot on your carpet with your old machine. The next step is to clean the same spot with his machine. Naturally he will get more dirt the second time. (He would with any machine.)

Then he asks, "Which machine would you rather have to clean your house?"

You have a free choice, but to select your old machine is to openly admit to being a careless housekeeper.

For the Biblical example, read Matthew 25:1-13.

Jesus uses the *Weighted Choice* in this story of the wise and foolish virgins. He would have us follow the practices of the wise ones, so he tells us which is which. It is not difficult to tell with whom to identify.

Like all good sales messages, this story is a powerful combination of several important techniques. Jesus uses at least three. We discuss the *Secret Identity* in chapter three. Later, in chapter six, we will discuss the *Fear of Loss*.

Here, we present Billy's Private Telephone Line To God. It combines the weighted choice with the story method of Secret Identity.

At first, we identify with Billy, and his choices become ours. Then things go wrong. We do not like the results. The choices are so weighted against Billy that we decide to take the alternate directions posed.

Billy's story can easily stand alone, but makes a more interesting performance if accompanied with actions. If you are a Christian performer, you will find that your favorite cut and restored rope trick adapts well to it.

BILLY'S PRIVATE TELEPHONE LINE TO GOD

When Billy was five years old, he thought he had a private telephone line to God. If he listened very closely he could hear God whisper to him in the treetops, and he could hear God speak out clearly in the bright colors of the flowers. Sometimes he thought he could even see God in the deep distant blue of the sky. Most important, Billy listened carefully to God speaking to him in the words of his parents and teachers.

And then Billy grew up to be ten years old. At ten Billy thought listening to God was kid stuff. Sometimes he stopped saying his prayers to God, and he did not listen quite as carefully to what his parents had to say to him. Sometimes he even wondered if it were really God whispering to him in the treetops. Maybe it was just the wind.

And Billy grew up to be fifteen. At fifteen, Billy decided he was tired of having God boss him around. He didn't need God to tell him what to do. He was big enough to take care of himself, and just to prove it; he cut his telephone line to God. He cut it completely in two. He did it by first refusing to say his prayers. He stopped going to church and he absolutely refused to listen to anything at all his parents had to say.

And Billy grew to be twenty—then twenty-five—and thirty.

He thought to himself, "This may be God's world, but I'm in charge of it now."

He looked up at the trees and laughed to think he could have ever been so silly as to believe he had heard God speaking there.

So he cut down all the trees and sold them for lumber. Then he took the money and built big shopping centers; and paved all the meadows to make parking lots.

And Billy grew older still.

As time went by, the rains came down and washed big gullys where the trees had been. The fumes from all the cars in the parking lots poisoned the air; and made life very difficult. Billy was old enough to have children of his own, and they could not find a grassy place in which to play.

And Billy grew very worried indeed. He was not sure he could solve these problems. Quickly he picked up his private telephone line to God and called for help. But he had forgotten that the telephone line was cut. He tried to tie the line back together again; but everyone knows you can't talk through a knot in a broken telephone line—not even to God. He thought about getting help from his parents; but Billy was too old to have parents who could fix everything. And Billy was old enough to know that there are some things that no human being can fix.

What was he to do? He ran around and around in circles trying to find an answer. Then one day, quite by accident, he found his way back to church. Perhaps it was just for a visit. There he discovered what he was looking for. He learned that there was only one way to repair a broken telephone line to God. He heard how God had sent Jesus, his son, to earth to make contact with all of those people who had lost touch with God.

Billy was happy and sad at the same time. He was happy, of course, because he had found the answer to his problem. He was sad because he saw all the unhappiness he had caused himself, and all of those around him. He made up his mind right there and then. He would never lose contact with God again.

5

SPECIAL INCENTIVE

For Me?

Our lives are filled with special offers of every kind. Parents sometimes offer an ice cream cone for good behavior, or cash for good grades. We give tips to waiters, and receive discounts from businesses of all sorts for purchasing certain products. Advertisers call this method of persuasion the *Special Incentive*. **You offer your listener a bonus if he will do what you ask.**

As you may already sense, there are some real pitfalls to be avoided in using this technique. Tips have become the expected thing, rather than a special incentive for extra service. Kids get so they won't cooperate without a bribe.

Advertisers tell us that to avoid such problems, the most effective incentives are those that are the most unrelated to the product. It is better to offer a trip to the local amusement park as a reward for saving grocery receipts, than it is to provide a year's supply of free groceries—even though the dollar value of the trip may be less than the free groceries.

The major reasons tipping has lost its effectiveness as a *Special Incentive*, is that it represents payment in kind. It has grown to be a substitute for a paycheck. It has become taken for granted.

To avoid this, financial institutions often offer merchandise (glassware, pens, restaurant credits, or even a prepaid cell phone) for investing.

To avoid the *Special Incentive* being taken as a bribe, some businesses give financial payment to a specified charity, instead of to the customer. It is a direction parents may want to consider to motivate their children. Children are very idealistic. Find out what charities turn them on. A few pennies set aside for starving children may be just the incentive they need to clean their plates.

As a Biblical example, we have selected Luke 12: 22-31(KJV). This talks of the lilies of the fields and how royally they are clothed.

Physical existence was hard in Bible times. There was no running water, no electricity, and no refrigeration. Food, drink, and, clothing were all concerns, but not intrinsic parts of the Kingdom. They are an unrelated extra bonus that God will provide. We are told to take care of the spirit, and all else will be added.

Here is a performance example. It has been written to be used with a magical effect called Six Bill Repeat. The trick is made up from stage money. If you want to use real money, or cannot find the bill trick, you can make it up from real money by following the pattern of the Six Card Repeat. The card trick should be easier to find.

HOW GOD CAN MULTIPLY MONEY

Once upon a time there was a man who worked very hard all week long. At the end of the week when he took home his pay, he had just barely enough to (counting off six bill as you go) keep food on the table, a shirt on his back, a roof over his head, fuel in the furnace, enough to pay the doctor, and still have some left over to put gas in the car for the next week. It was a wearisome way to live and he was not happy. He looked around and saw that this was a beautiful world, and he wanted to enjoy it just a bit. He also saw that God had given him a fine family and strength to earn the few dollars he brought home each week. He wanted somehow to show his gratitude, but there never seemed to be anything left.

One Sunday morning as the collection plate came by; he said to himself, "I've been getting a little broad around the middle lately. I'll eat just a little less next week," and he put a whole dollar in the collection plate (toss one bill aside.) That night, when he sat down to divide his money for next week, he discovered he had (again counting six bills) just barely enough to put food on the table, keep a shirt on his back (etc. through the six bills).

He was so surprised and so excited that next Sunday—without even thinking about it—(toss 2 bills this time) he put in two bills instead of just one.

"Now, I'm really in trouble," he thought. But next week he walked to a few places instead of driving. He was even a little healthier that way, and as time went by he needed less to pay the doctor. Each week he always seemed to have just enough left over to keep food on the table, etc. (counting through six bills.)

"My goodness," he thought. "This is very surprising and exciting. I must tell others about this." Next Sunday he put three bills into the collection plate to help spread the good news. (Toss away three bills.)

That's when he discovered the strangest thing of all. He found that his life had lost its dullness. He discovered that he had just enough to put food on the table, a shirt on his back, a roof overhead, fuel in the furnace, pay the doctor bill, and put gas in the car. What's more he still had enough left over (counting three additional bills for a total of nine) to share the joy of God's world, do nice things for other people, and put a smile on his own face too.

6

FEAR OF LOSS

Oh no you don't

At first glance, *Fear of Loss* seems to be almost the same as the *Special Incentive*. Certainly, if you do not take advantage of any special offers made, obviously you will have lost them. But losing what one has never had, is not nearly as painful as losing what one already owns. **Fear of Loss threatens your listener with loosing something he already possesses.**

For example, suppose I woke you from a sound sleep to give you a hundred dollar bill. You would probably mutter something like "Go away. I'll deal with that in the morning." On the other hand, if I woke you up by taking a similar amount from your wallet, you would likely be alert instantly, ready to defend. That is the power of *Fear of Loss*. It is probably the most powerful motivating force among the tools of persuasion, but it is extremely negative.

Since it is so negative, special care must be taken to avoid using it as a threat or punishment. It is an important distinction to make. It is the crucial difference between the helpfulness of the true salesman, and the hurrangs and shouts, coercion and arm-twisting of the hucksters and pulpit-pounders.

In the Bible, John the Baptist threatens, scolds, and accuses. He assumes the listeners have already lost the Kingdom, and will be punished for it. As a result, he antagonizes his listeners and his message is lost.

In contrast, Jesus avoids using the *Fear of Loss* whenever possible. He starts with the assumption that we possess the Kingdom of God. He assumes the best of us. (See Chapter two, *Assuming the Desired Result.*) In Luke 14: 7-11 (KJV), He uses the *Special Incentive* instead. The story is about seating around a dinner table; but it deals with being in line for the kingdom. He tells the story of certain people crowding to the head of the table. Instead of belittling his characters for being pushy, he assumes the best of them. He assumes they just do not know proper etiquette, and provides them with that information. If they go to the foot of the table, they almost certainly will be given the privilege of moving up. He makes what could be a threat of losing the kingdom, into a way of gaining the kingdom.

Never the less, *Fear of Loss* was certainly a major tool in Jesus' persuasions. In Luke 12:13-21(KJV), Jesus tells the story of the man who tears down his old barns in order to build bigger ones. Jesus uses the *Fear of Loss* of eternal life to counter the man's *Fear of Loss* of physical security. Evidently, Jesus feels that he needs to fight one fear with a stronger fear.

Though powerful, this technique is so painful that it is hard to find a contemporary example. Most advertisers do not want to associate their products with causing pain. The exceptions are negative political ads. These ads are designed to engender fear of what would happen if the other candidate won. We all deplore this type of ad, but the fact remains that they are enormously persuasive. Here is one non-political radio commercial that uses *The Fear of Loss* as its main persuasive tool. Just thirty seconds of airtime was all it took to shake its listeners to their very foundations.

It starts with a quiet voice heard as if in the mind of the speaker.

"Oh, I'm sick . . . so sick . . . can't get sick . . .

Not enough money . . . might get laid off and then what?

Not enough money . . . wish I'd saved . . . wish I'd saved . . . too late . . . too late . . .

Then a kindly voice says, "It's not too late if you start now to save at ABC Savings. They offer a full X% interest etc."

This very short commercial was aired only a few times before it brought in new savers by the droves. They were angry, irritated, and upset. They demanded that the advertiser take those blankety-blank commercials off the air. Then they quietly opened a new account and walked out.

Because *Fear of Loss* is so powerful, and has an element of threat to it, we have chosen not to include a performance example. A performance, by its very nature, needs to be entertaining rather than threatening. Instead, and before moving on, we need to demonstrate how the various techniques can become more powerful by using them together. Lets suppose we are planning a shopping trip with a fifteen-year-old girl. Before even setting a date, we have set the stage. We used the *Secret Identity* along with humor and excitement, to tell a story about an earlier successful shopping trip with someone else. The story would have emphasized the behaviors we expect, but in no way should our young lady be led to believe it is about or relates to her. It should be presented merely as an entertaining story.

We start the actual trip by assuming the best. We assume she is courteous, intelligent, fun loving, and cooperative. In one-way or another, we let our young lady know that we recognize all these good qualities about her. No doubt she will be complimented and try to live up to our expectations. Later, if any of our assumptions are contradicted, we never scold or get angry. Instead, we deal with it by assuming that our young lady got tired, did not understand, or just forgot how to behave properly. To provide extra insurance that our assumptions will be met, we use the *Special Incentive*, by hinting at a surprise to come at the end of a good trip. We only offer it. We do not use it as a bribe, or as a threat of withdrawal later.

To divert attention from possible misbehavior, and to guide us through the day, we give our young lady *Simple and Weighted Choices* of what activities we might pursue. This gives her input; but either way she chooses, the choices we give her will work for us, too.

Finally at the end of the day, the special surprise is provided, or forgotten, as the case may require.

7

THE RULE OF PHYSICAL ACTION

Don't stop me now

There is a universal rule of physical action quoted by many disciplines. Recently, a national drug company quoted it to advertise their painkiller. According to the rule, "Objects in motion tend to stay in motion. Objects at rest tend to stay at rest."

In fact, this rule is also a persuasive technique called the rule of *Physical Action*. **In this method, you start your listener moving in the direction you want him to go, and enable him to keep on going.** The secret is to get them started.

In the Bible, check out John 9: 6-7 (KJV). This is the incident in which Jesus heals the blind man by applying mud to his eyes. The man is told to wash it off in a certain near by body of water. Since the mud must be removed in some way, the rule of *Physical Action* is brought into play. It takes very little additional energy or faith to go the extra steps to the designated location. It would not have been so easy if Jesus had merely told the man to apply the mud to his own eyes.

Today, makers of products sometimes offer a free trial package. The action of using free sample seems to be no commitment at all, but the fact is that it establishes a small habit in the desired direction. If the manufacturer also gets you to accept an extra amount off on your next purchase, the habit is firmly established. It is easier to keep using the product than it is to change.

Here is another subtler example. Suppose a salesman sits talking with you in your living room. His pen accidentally (?) falls to the floor. Not seeming to notice, he continues to talk. Being a courteous host, you pick up the pen. He allows you to fiddle with it for a few moments before noticing.

Then taking your action as impatience he says, "Oh, I'm sorry. Here's the contract. You can sign right here."

At this point, it is easier for you to sign than not to sign. An object in motion continues to stay in motion, etc . . .

This method works especially well in small groups and on a one-to-one basis. It is harder to manage with large audiences, but here is a method which one pastor used. He gave each of his congregation a dollar bill and commissioned them to use it as in the parable of the talents. The ways in which his flock found to multiply the dollars were ingenious. More important for them, it set the rule of *Physical Action* to work in their lives, teaching stewardship by doing.

The following is a good example for the performer to use. The only difficulty here is that it requires the audience to transfer their understandings from the pretend situation into their daily lives.

LET'S PLAY GOD

ACTION: The magician holds a ball in his hand. An audience member holds the magician's wrist, so that the ball cannot go up his sleeve. The ball is then covered with a handkerchief and various audience members feel the ball to make sure it is still there. Magic words are said, and when the handkerchief is removed, the ball is gone.

METHOD: The last person to feel the ball is a secret assistant and removes it secretly. Though the trick may be accomplished other ways, the use of the secret assistant is important to the message. A magician's sponge ball is ideal to use because it looks big, but compresses easily for hiding.

MESSAGE: "Here in my hand is the world and I am God. I know that's hard to believe, but if a movie star can do it, I guess I can too. Today, I am going to make the world disappear—with your help, of course. God often likes to work through other people.

"First, I hold the world in my left hand. My goodness, there seems to be a dark spot right on my hometown. Maybe it's going to rain.

"Now, just to prove it's a real miracle and nothing goes up my sleeve, will you hold my wrist?"

Select someone for this purpose.

"Next, we'll cover the world with my handkerchief and the rest of you feel under the handkerchief, one at a time, to make sure the world is still there. Very good. Now I will wave my wand. What? No thunder? We must have thunder. Everyone stamp your feet when I wave my wand. With that, the world has vanished."

Remove the handkerchief to show your empty hand.

"Would you like to know how I, as God, did that miracle? I'll show you. Correction, Mary (secret assistant's name) will show you."

Have your secret assistant stand up and show the ball.

"Mary did what God, that's me, asked her to do. She secretly took the ball and let me, as God, take the credit.

"Actually, we all did it. You did the believing. Mary did what God asked and let me, as God, take the credit. Without all of us doing our part, no one would have been amazed. That's how we all perform miracles for God everyday, some-times without even knowing it."

8

REQUEST FOR ACTION

I thought you'd never ask

Closing a sale is like a marriage proposal. **A definite question needs to be asked in order for the listener to respond with a definite answer.** This is true whether the persuasion regards a product, a philosophy, or a behavior. For the purposes of easy discussion, we shall limit ourselves mainly to product sales. By now you should have sufficient information to make adaptations on your own.

For many a salesman, popping the critical question is as scary as making a marriage proposal; but it is absolutely essential to making a sale. Quite unlike a marriage proposal, even a "no" answer can be the key to making the sale.

One more little question may be all it takes. The question is "Why not?" Once you know why not, you can concentrate on what other persuasive technique will work best to close the sale. Soon you will be ready to ask the question again.

Each persuasive technique provides its own unique way to ask for the order. In this chapter, let us examine some of those ways.

We will begin with *Assuming the Desired Result*, which in this case means assuming they are going to buy. Still, the question as to whether to buy or not has to be asked, otherwise it's like the engaged couple who never sets the date. You might begin the questioning with, "Judging from what you told me, I would guess you would want the deluxe model. Am I right?"

Notice the question after the statement. It is important to get a definite commitment. This might be followed with, "When would you like to have it delivered?"

Other questions, which might be asked, are: "Will this be cash or charge?" "Do you want the one with the left or right-hand door?"

Notice that these questions ask for a definite answer. Obviously you cannot close a sale unless the customer agrees. These questions are also excellent examples of how to close by means of *The Choice*.

The *Secret Identity* is a good technique to use if a customer has already said "no." Once you know your customer's objections, you can weave them into a story. For example: "Just the other day, an earlier customer expressed some of these same concerns. Here's what he did. Is that something which would work for you?"

The *Special Incentive* works well if you save it to the very end as a closing technique. When you are ready to close, you can say, "If you purchase through me now, I can give you X% discount. Shall I write up the order?"

To add extra urgency, you can easily turn this into *Fear of Loss* by putting a time limit on the offer.

As to the Rule of *Physical Action*, anything you can do to let the customer handle or use the product is valuable. This does not replace asking specifically for your customer to commit to a purchase, but a test drive, a free trial offer, even a hand held examination will accomplish much toward that end.

9

QUICK-FIX SHORT CUTS

Before you dive in head first to make the persuasive techniques work for you, it would be a good idea to do a little advance preparation. We have all done a goodly number of things from time to time that have put some barriers between ourselves and our family, friends, and fellow workers. It's a good idea to repair a few bridges before trying to sell them on your ideas. A salesman, most of all, needs to be liked and trusted. There are a few short cuts you can take in advance to make that happen. In a sense, they parallel the *Persuasive Techniques,* or are persuasive in and of themselves. They are also much simpler and easier to handle. It is good training to start here first. Then refer back to the persuasive techniques.

INDIRECT PRESENTATION OF IDEAS

1. **Take good intentions for granted.** (Check Chapter two) In this case, you do not have a specific action you would have your listener follow. Your only concern is to recognize his good points. To quote an old adage, "It takes a dozen at-a-boys to counter balance one criticism." You will be amazed at what an impression you make when you openly recognize his good points:

2. **Credit another when he happens to make the desired response:** When you honestly brag on someone, his or her ego is boosted a thousand fold. Do this a few times to

someone you want to change, and you could sell him the Brooklyn Bridge.

3. **Credit another with your own idea**: Be careful here, don't misquote him, but you might say, "John has a wonderful idea. As I understand, it had to do with . . ." If you do it right, he is likely to accept your statement of his idea as his own.

4. **Giving facts without drawing conclusions**: This is very similar to the *Weighted Choice* in Chapter four. Be sure you are fair in listing the facts. When the evidence is fully laid out, it may easily cause others to change their minds.

5. **Ask it as a question.** Stating your idea as a statement has a way of sounding like an edict from on high. Asking it as a question signals the listener that you are open to other ideas, and causes him to formulate a more complete answer of his own. It may also open the discussion to new ideas not explored before. You could say, "What do you think about doing it this way?" Then state your idea.

DIRECT PRESENTATION OF IDEAS

Sometimes it is best to present your ideas directly. This is a democracy and the best solutions come from airing all points of view. Here are some ideas toward that direction. The first and second suggestions sort of go together, one after the other.

1. **Encourage others to express their opinion**: As a chairman, this is easy. If you are a member of the group, you may need to gain the floor to say things like "So and so had something rather important to say on this subject." In working with one of your children, ask, "Tell me what you think should be done in this case." When you express respect for other people's ideas, they will be more open to yours.

2. **Express a concern that your thoughts also need to be heard**: Once others have had a chance to say what's on their mind, they are going to be more willing to listen to your ideas. You could start by asking "May I also say a few words on the subject?" or "Several of you have asked for my opinion as well. May I express it now?"

3. **Act as a spokesman for others**: In this case you need not have specific people in mind for which you are speaking, though it is certainly a good idea. The fact is that if your ideas are good, others will have thought of them as well. Acting as a spokesman conveys the idea that you do not necessarily endorse the idea, so it avoids a direct confrontation. It also suggests other support for your ideas.

4. **Present an idea as being a good policy**: Instead of attacking the individual for not doing the right thing, this puts it in general, non-personal terms. You could say "It is a good idea to . . ."; "It pays to . . ."; "It is the thing to do . . ."; "A person never goes wrong by . . ."

5. **State that *we* should do a certain thing:** This accomplishes the same purpose as number four above, but adds extra strength to the statement. It's hard to argue with someone who is on your team.

INOFFENSIVE OPPOSITION TO IDEAS

A person's ideas are a part of themselves. They are brainchildren, so to speak. Disrespect the ideas and you show disrespect to the person. Many of these techniques are almost self-explanatory, but they all convey respect in some way.

1. **Make a concession before rejecting an idea.** When you make a concession, you show that you recognize that there is at least some truth in what he says, and thus you take

the sting out of your rejection. Try comments like "Much might be said on either side." "Under normal conditions your idea is a good one, but this is an unusual situation." "We agree in essentials. We differ only in details."

2. **Take a deliberative attitude before rejecting the idea.** By considering the idea to begin with, it can be rejected later with less danger of offending. This method is not only a good one from the standpoint of persuasion, but it also conveys a special respect and courtesy for its own sake.

3. **State that there are others who agree before disagreeing.** Any statement, which indicates that others may agree, acts as a buffer later, if the idea must be rejected. This technique may be used in reverse. You state your agreement but indicate that others will not agree, and therefore the idea will not pass muster.

4. **Restate the individual's idea and ask him if that is what he meant.** Most people speak carelessly and say more than they mean. By repeating it back to him, you can often get him to change his stand in the direction of a more moderate view.

5. **Excuse a person from blame for the idea he has expressed.** Notice that in a goodly number of the following quotes, you assume part of the responsibility for the miscommunication, even though you may not be to blame. At least you can give the other person the benefit of the doubt. Many an argument can be avoided with statements like these. "You couldn't have known this, but . . ." "I don't think I made it clear. What I meant to say was . . ." "I believe that we are looking at this from different angles." "I may have given you the wrong idea here."

6. **Refrain from being over positive.** Over positive statements come across as being bigoted and over bearing. Instead, use

such comments as: "I am inclined to think otherwise." "You may be right, but I can't quite see it that way." "I didn't get that impression."

7. **Pay tribute to the individual before objecting.** Many people are objective enough to understand that an attack on an idea is not an attack on them, but some do not. To avoid this, you can acknowledge his personal qualities first, before evaluating the idea. For example, "Son, you are a bright young man, but I disagree with you on this one."

8. **Go lightly banter.** By sharing a laugh before hand, you can create a feeling of good-natured fellowship. The criticism will come across much more easily. Recently, I had to call a friend with a rather serious complaint. I left a message and when he called me back, I was on the john. Laughingly I said "John, you caught me on the john. I hope you don't mind the play on words," and the ice was broken. We both had a good laugh and the criticism went down quite easily.

THE BEST IDEA OF ALL:

Keep in mined that the techniques offered in this book are not hard and fast rules. They are merely suggestions, ways and means to help bring about a final solution that is acceptable to all. To paraphrase a line from our very first chapter, "A real salesman has the customer's needs at heart, not strictly his own. He is kind, considerate, tells the truth, and sincerely wants to help. It is for our own best interests, as well as his, that he wants us to make a change."

ABOUT THE AUTHOR

R W (Bob) Klamm was born in 1930 in Kansas City KS. No one knew he was nearly blind until he was eight years old and they caught him cheating on the flash cards.

He continued to struggle through normal school, and then Services for the Blind sent him to Northwestern University, where he graduated "with distinction" in Communications.

He returned to KC and began a career in advertising. The industry was on the brink of a movement toward subliminal psychology. As a writer for Standart & O'Hern Advertising, a Kansas City MO based firm, Mr. Klamm pioneered the use of psychological methods in radio, TV, and print. Before long, his work was singled out for recognition and study by a major New York agency.

His experience in magic extends back some 38 years. For 20 years he taught high school persuasive speech, theater, and debate. In addition, he has received two awards for original radio drama, written several books on magic, is a long-standing Methodist, a member of the Fellowship of Christian Magicians, and an Elder in the Presbyterian Church.

Samples of his other writings can be found on his two web sites. Bob enjoys talking with readers about it all.

klamm-magic.com
klammbooks.com

816-254-0432

APPENDIX

Klamm Magic LLC
1412 S Appleton Ave
Independence MO 64052
816-461-4595
klamm-magic.com
klamm@klamm-magic.com

U.S. Toy
2008 W 103rd Terrace
Leawood KS 66206
913-642-8247 (Magic Shop)
ustoy.com (Search Magic Tricks)

Magic Supply Company
(On line only)
magicsupply.com
1-877-280-7900

Printed in the United States
By Bookmasters

Starlit

Also by Lisa Rinna

RINNAVATION

Starlit

A Novel

LISA RINNA

Pocket Books

New York • London • Toronto • Sydney

Pocket Books
A Division of Simon & Schuster, Inc.
1230 Avenue of the Americas
New York, NY 10020

This book is a work of fiction. Names, characters, places, and incidents either are products of the author's imagination or are used fictitiously. Any resemblance to actual events or locales or persons, living or dead, is entirely coincidental.

First Pocket Books paperback edition September 2011

POCKET and colophon are registered trademarks of Simon & Schuster, Inc.

For information about special discounts for bulk purchases, please contact Simon & Schuster Special Sales at 1-866-506-1949 or business@simonandschuster.com.

The Simon & Schuster Speakers Bureau can bring authors to your live event. For more information or to book an event contact the Simon & Schuster Speakers Bureau at 1-866-248-3049 or visit our website at www.simonspeakers.com.

Cover photo by Evan Schwartz

Manufactured in the United States of America

10 9 8 7 6 5 4 3 2 1

ISBN 978-1-4767-8833-3

To my husband,

"I'd be lost without you baby"

Starlit

Chapter 1

OSCAR NIGHT WAS breezy and starlit, both outside the Sunset Tower in Beverly Hills, where the *Vanity Fair* party was in full swing, and inside as well.

Even before the Academy Awards broadcast began, an endless procession of limousines had been arriving at the hotel for the invitation-only dinner that took place before the magazine's renowned after party. All evening long, as stars, auteurs, moguls, trendsetters, and celebutants hit the *VF* red carpet, an army of paparazzi surged against the black velvet rope. Granted, the photographers knew better than to cross it, but that didn't stop them from begging for those laser-bright smiles from J Lo, Stiller or Meryl, or either Gyllenhaal.

The shout-outs from 'razzis and the thunderous clicks of camera shutters were maddening. Those less practiced at being in the public eye—Oscar first-timers, agents, plus ones, or the errant producers whose previous or current films rated a golden ticket to the party—either scowled or blinked like deer caught in headlights. But for those who really mattered, delivering the money shot was a cakewalk. Their customized red-carpet pap struts had been drilled into them by years of practice with image consultants. For the men, it was a relaxed stance with one hand in a pocket, a sly grin, and a casual wave. The starlets knew to come to a complete stop over the *VF* logo stamped dead center on the candy-apple red carpet, then do a half-turn, with breasts thrust forward and lips poised in a come-hither smile. Even as their Bluetoothed handlers hustled them inside, the photos were uplinked to the Internet so that the rest of the world could drool over the ultimate Hollywood experience.

And tonight Tally Jones was right in the middle of it all.

The fact that she was wearing not a designer gown but a crisp white shirt and black slacks like all the other waiters didn't matter. Nor did it bother her that every other actor in the room had a more successful career than hers.

OK, so maybe it was making her feel a *little* insecure. "We just have to remind ourselves that this is only a temporary gig," she murmured under her breath, as much to herself as to her friends, Sadie Fletcher and Mandy Hogan, who stood beside her there in the center of the massive ballroom. "Positive thinking, right? Otherwise, we'll never be here again. Unless it's to pass cheeseburgers to the stars."

When Sadie's boss, the hotel's owner, Jeff Klein, had announced that additional cater-waiters would be needed for the event, Sadie had seen to it that Tally and Mandy were hired on. All night long, Sadie and Mandy had circulated with trays of crystal flutes filled with champagne, whereas Tally's job was to pass around cheeseburgers from the platter she carried. But amid the pulsating strobe lights, the loud thumping music, the hustle and flow of the crowd (not to mention the fact that *Yes, omigod*, that *is* Tom Hanks, standing *right there* within spitting distance, can you *believe* it?), every hour or so, the girls sought one another out not only to catch their breath but to pinch themselves at their great luck to be there.

Inevitably, though, one of them would sigh and ask, "When will it be our turn?" This time, it was Mandy. "I hope you're right, Tally. But I've been in Hollywood for three years now. Sadie's been auditioning for five. I'd say we're all due for a break, don't you think?"

From the scowl on Sadie's face, Tally knew that

nothing she could say would make her friend feel any less anxious about their immediate situation. Since having met in acting class two years ago, none of them had scored more than a walk-on or a crowd shot in an indie flick.

"Let's face facts, Tally," Sadie said flatly. "Kate Winslet had already made *Titanic* by the time she was our age, and Jessica Alba was starring in *Dark Angel*! By those standards, we're already has-beens."

"Don't be silly," Tally murmured, and smiled sweetly as Russell Crowe and some cute nobody with a scruffy beard grabbed two burgers off her tray. She waited until the men moved on before resuming scolding her pal. "No pity parties, Sadie. Look, how can we be has-beens? Really, we're *never*-beens." Seeing the alarm in Mandy's eyes, she quickly added, "No, make that *haven't-been-yets*. We have talent, now we just need a little luck."

"OK, now I need a drink." Mandy glanced around quickly. Noting that Jeff was nowhere in sight, she ducked behind a pillar and gulped two quick swigs of champagne from one of the glasses on her tray. But any comfort she got from it was gone a second later, when she spied a trio of starlets making their way over to the ladies' room. "Oh my God! Did you get a good look at Scarlett Johansson's dress? If they gave out an Oscar for Best Cleavage, she'd win, hands down." Mandy glared down at her own meager chest. At home in Cleveland, her sunny smile and pencil-slim golden-girl-next-door looks had gotten her every role she'd ever gone out for. But here in LA, "pretty" hadn't landed her one walk-on in a commercial, let alone a movie or a TV series.

She groaned. "I just realized why that casting director last week called me 'boyishly trim.' That's got to be 'flat-chested' in Hollywood-speak. I guess I should start saving for a boob job."

"Don't be so hard on yourself." Tally patted her on the shoulder. "Some of the best actresses in the world are thin. Look at Nicole and Renée."

"That's easy for you to say," Mandy sniffed.

Unlike Mandy's, Tally's breasts were generous. She was also slender and broad-shouldered, with well-chiseled cheekbones, a pert nose, and thick auburn hair that curled down to her shoulders. And, like most of the women in the restaurant, Mandy and Sadie would have given anything to have Tally's perfect Cupid's bow of a mouth, something their friend was too modest to appreciate. Whenever Tally smiled, the happiness on her naturally full lips seemed to light up her almond-shaped, caramel-hued eyes.

"She's right." Sadie sighed. "Tally, if I were you, I would have been discovered at, like, age two." Despite having grown up in Los Angeles's San Fernando Valley, Sadie was the antithesis of the proverbial Valley girl. She was plump, with frizzy red hair, freckles, and a nose with a tiny bump that the other girls assured her gave her face character.

Tally smiled as George Lucas plucked a burger off her platter. She was about to ask him if it was true that he was in preproduction with *Star Wars VII, VIII*, and *IX*, but she came to her senses and stopped herself. Like every other waiter hired for the event, she had been forewarned not to gawk and to keep circulating with her tray of appetizers. Having a shot at being listed in the credits as the third Ewok on the right wasn't worth risking the best gig she'd gotten in LA thus far.

While she hadn't yet been discovered by someone who could help her career, tonight she was getting up close and personal with many of her favorite stars. And, professional demeanor aside, she kept her eyes open for any possible souvenirs to put in her "My Life in Hollywood" scrapbook. Like the Kleenex Halle Berry had used to blot her lipstick (was it really Revlon Super Lustrous Mulled Wine? Tally made herself a promise to compare it with the samples at the makeup counter at CVS) and the empty Tic Tacs box Robert Downey Jr. had placed on her tray with an apologetic shrug.

But it was Sadie who landed the big prize of the night. "Don't say I never gave you anything," she muttered as she slipped a swizzle stick onto Tally's platter.

Tally looked down at it, puzzled. "OK, why did you just do that?"

"Because it just came out of George Clooney's mouth! It was stuck in the olive that was in his martini."

Tally was so excited she almost dropped her tray.

"And don't look now, but Johnny Depp is headed outside for a smoke with Sean Penn." Sadie jerked her head toward the restaurant's rooftop deck. "They might leave behind a matchbook. Do yourself a favor, and see if they're into cheeseburgers."

Tally shook her head. "If they're smoking, they won't want to eat."

"You're right." Mandy pushed her tray forward. "But they might want a drink. Here, swap with me."

Tally shot her friend a grateful smile. Balancing the tray precariously on her arm, she made her way gingerly through the crowd and out the door.

"Every beautiful woman in the world is right here, but you've been staring at that cute little waitress all night." Josh Gold snapped his fingers in front of his friend's eyes. "What, does she remind you of your very first girlfriend or something? I'm guessing you haven't heard a word I've said in the past ten minutes."

"Huh? Oh . . . yeah, sorry," Mac Carlton said apologetically.

Josh might have been one of the most powerful agents in Hollywood, but whatever he was harping about wasn't so important that Mac felt he had to stop admiring the view. Josh was right about one thing, though: of all the beautiful girls at the party, the only one he wanted to meet was lugging around a tray of cheeseburgers.

Already, he'd eaten three of them. But had she even noticed him? Nah, he doubted it. Sure, she'd tossed off one of those dazzling smiles and made polite chitchat while handing him a napkin, but he could see she'd been too busy trying not to stare at all the stars to register his presence. Not that he could blame her. Toned, buffed up, and dressed in a tux, even the surliest actor was guy candy to a starstruck civilian.

A regular guy like me doesn't have much of a chance, Mac thought, figuring it'd be better just to bide his time. Tomorrow he would stop by and coerce Jeff into giving him her number.

As if reading his mind, Josh let out a loud snort. "Come on, already, you and I both know that power is the greatest aphrodisiac." Josh pointed to Mac's Oscar, which had been placed prominently on the shelf behind their banquette. "Dude, just show her this, and game over."

"What would be the fun in that?" Mac smiled and thoughtfully scratched his beard. It was a souvenir from Alaska, where he'd spent the last month holding the hands of the first-time director and the temperamental lead actress who were shooting the current project he had in production. He'd landed back in Los Angeles just a few hours before the ceremony. He wished he'd had a few minutes to shave, but he'd barely had time to throw on a tux and make it to the Kodak Theater in time to receive his award. "I'm a romantic. For once, I want a woman to love me for my wit, charm, and good looks as opposed to who I am. Not another starlet who dates me because she thinks I'll put her in my next picture, but a normal, everyday girl. Like *her*." He nodded toward Tally. "She seems . . . perfect."

Josh laughed so hard at this that he almost choked on his drink. "Well, if she's going to fall for your looks, then you'd better go into the men's room and shave. Beards haven't been sexy since the Bee Gees had a disco hit. Hey, speaking of hit-making foreigners we all adore, it looked like Russell was all ears just now when you two were talking. So, does he want to do that movie you're shooting in Paris next summer? Because Angelina and I have been feeling each other out since she walked from her agency. If Russell's a go, I could use that as leverage with her—"

"Actually, I was talking to Russell about something else. He's been approached by Scorsese to star in the remake of *Double Indemnity*, and as much as he'd like to consider the role, he was grousing about my father's treatment of him on his last film—and from what he says, he means his *very* last film—with Royalton, so he might turn it down."

Josh smirked knowingly. Mac's father, Richard, was the chairman of Royalton Studios and its largest stockholder as well. The movies it produced were big-budget blockbusters—although these days, Royalton was spending more on its movies than the returns it was seeing at the box office. "Well, your dad has always been a ball-busting son of a bitch. That's why you flew the coop in the first place, right? And Crowe certainly isn't known to back down from a fight, particularly when he believes in something."

"Russell *is* interested in the part and in working with Marty. He asked me to have a word with dear old Dad, and I was trying to explain to him that it probably wouldn't help. After all, if Richard and I saw eye-to-eye on this business, I'd be sharing this hunk of brass with Royalton."

Josh grabbed the Oscar statuette and lifted it like a barbell. "Boy, after tonight, I'll bet your old man wishes you'd stayed put as the president of his studio's movie division." He put a napkin to his nose and sneezed. Periodically throughout the night, Josh had been making pit stops in the john. He was a renowned cokehead, but he was also one of the town's biggest agents, so, like everyone else, Mac put up with Josh's bad habits.

Mac shrugged and took the statue. Yes, its weight was impressive, but he was more in awe of what it symbolized. Having just had the project he'd been babying for the past three years win the Best Picture Oscar, he had every reason to be crowing tonight and not giving his father's troubles a second thought. But that was hard to do when his mentor—in Mac's case, Richard—hadn't even had the decency to rise from his seat and clap him on the back as he'd made his way onto the stage. He hadn't sought him out at the party, to tell him how proud he was of his son, either. Instead, Richard and Mac's mother, Elizabeth—one of Royalton's last contract players and still considered a Hollywood grande dame—had made it a point to keep out of their only child's way all evening long.

That was fine with Mac. His father was a dinosaur who had long needed a reality check, and the sooner that happened, the better, though not necessarily tonight. For the next hour or so, Mac planned on enjoying this glittering fairy tale he knew too well, as viewed through the large, limpid eyes of a girl who hungered to be a part of it. That is, if he could find her again.

Tuning out Josh's babbling, he scanned the crowded room, but the lighting was so soft he couldn't find the waitress with the luscious lips anywhere. Finally, he spotted her switching trays with one of the other waitresses and heading out to the rooftop deck.

Mac shoved the Oscar at Josh. "Here, stash this somewhere. I need some fresh air."

With that, Mac weaved his way through the thick throng of back slappers, well-wishers, and envious peers who, he knew, swore under their breath that, at least tonight, he was the luckiest bastard in Hollywood.

We'll see about that, he thought.

Chapter 2

THE LIMOUSINE TAKING "the queen of nighttime serials" (at least, according to *People* magazine), Susie Sheppard, and her Oscar date, movie director Calvin Walsh, from the Governors Ball to the *Vanity Fair* party was moving at a snail's pace, with the rest of the star convoy headed in the same direction.

That was perfectly fine with Susie. From the looks of things, she'd need every minute of the ride to convince Calvin that she'd be the perfect lead for his next film, an updated version of *M*A*S*H*. Already, *Variety* was calling the project, *M*A*S*H*U*P*, a surefire blockbuster, noting how the television series catapulted Alan Alda and other members of the show's cast to stardom. Now, a whole generation later, it was time to do it all over again. And Susie Sheppard was determined to be the new Margaret "Hot Lips" Houlihan.

Granted, five years as the queen bee on her prime-time serial, *Dana Point*, had made her what she was today. But by Hollywood standards, that was still too far away from the best roles and the biggest paydays. To get to the next level, she knew she had to be the kind of actress whom directors thought of first and wanted the most. And, unfortunately for her, Susie's technique in front of the camera wasn't going to get her there.

Her best tricks weren't up her sleeve but between her legs. Or between her lips.

In the ten-plus years she'd been knocking around Hollywood, her method for staying first and foremost in a director's mind was tried and true, and she was employing it now with Calvin. Not that he was making it easy for her. In fact, Susie had been down on her knees—literally as well as figuratively—since the limo had turned onto Fairfax from Hollywood Boulevard.

It didn't help that Calvin's member was undersized to begin with. To make matters worse, no matter how much sucking and pumping she'd done, he'd stayed soft for the first five minutes she'd worked on him. She presumed it had to do with the fact that he was overworked, overweight, and over fifty, but to give him the benefit of the doubt, she was willing to buy into his excuse that he was devastated over losing the Best Director Oscar yet again. But, hey, everyone knew he was the long shot, right? So it had to be something else. One thing Susie knew for sure, from experience: it certainly wasn't her technique.

She always carried Vitamin V in her purse, but somehow, knowing the dude had popped a baby blue made it seem like cheating, so she hated to dole them out. In this case, there wasn't enough time, anyway. They were only a few minutes from their destination, and they'd be laughingstocks if he walked into the party with a tent in his pants. Well, if all else failed, she'd put a Mentos in her mouth. That always did the trick.

Luckily, it was soon evident that wasn't necessary, because by the time they turned onto Santa Monica Boulevard, she had her validation: he was stiff and stoked. *Thank God.*

She could tell he was close to coming, too, because he'd finally shut up about all the changes he'd made to the latest draft of *M*A*S*H*U*P*, such as moving the story locale to Iraq and making Corporal Klinger a full-blown Don't Ask Don't Tell tranny. As she swallowed and smiled, he gasped. "I'm going to have to give Hot Lips more scenes! A *helluva lot* more scenes."

"And lots of close-ups. Right, big boy?" She pressed her palm hard against his pants as she zipped him up slowly.

"Yeah . . . yeah! *Whatever!*" Calvin groaned so loudly the limo driver glanced in the rearview mirror. Susie caught his eye and gave him a wink. *Too bad for him,* she thought. Had Calvin not folded, she would have slipped the driver a note suggesting he swing by her place after he dropped off Calvin at home later that evening. But now that Calvin was committed, she'd certainly be going home with him. Tonight and every night until shooting began.

With her mission accomplished, she made a mental note to have her agent, Josh Gold, call him in the morning to finalize negotiations.

Susie shook her head sadly, thinking about how she was going to be spending her nights leading up to the shoot. Why couldn't Calvin have been better endowed? Oh, well. Once they started production, she'd find some willing playmates on the set.

Here's hoping my costars are straight, she thought. *The male ones, anyway.*

She leaned back, satisfied. There was certainly an advantage to swinging both ways.

Susie was still touching up her lipstick when they pulled up in front of the Sunset Tower. As soon as the limo came to a complete stop, a car crashed into them from behind, tossing her onto the floor of the car, Calvin on top of her. They could hear people screaming outside as they both scrambled onto the backseat, but neither of them realized that Calvin's shoe was wrapped in the train of her Versace gown until they heard the loud *rip*.

"Son of a *bitch*!" she cursed, but he was laughing, to the point where she thought he'd bust a gut. She couldn't understand why. Calvin was just about to tell her when the back door flew open on her side.

"I *knew* it! You bitch! I couldn't believe it when I saw you on the TV sitting beside this old asshole at the freakin' Oscars!" Jared Connolly didn't wait for Susie to reply before lunging over her toward Calvin.

Susie sighed in disgust. Like Jared, many of her other lovers got upset when she walked out on them. Sure, it hurt, but they eventually manned up and moved on. At only twenty-three, Jared had been her youngest conquest, at least since she'd turned thirty-five (and that was in *real* years, not the age she claimed to be in public). Sure, she'd had fun with him. Heck, he'd had more staying power than any other manboy she'd known—and that was saying a lot, considering her cougar status among Hollywood's young community of stud-pup actors. But two weeks ago, she'd set her sights on *M*A*S*H*U*P* and Calvin, and she hadn't returned Jared's calls since. That was life; business trumped pleasure. Good-bye, Eveready; hello, sore jaw.

Jared had taken her kiss-off particularly badly.

Already, she'd had to change her cell number because he called constantly and left heartbroken messages. She'd also beefed up the security at her place in Bel Air because of the many times she'd found him waiting for her outside her gate. She'd even had Jared banned from the set of *Dana Point*, but he always found a way to sneak onto it anyway, since his show, the teen drama *Valley Boys*, was also shot on the Royalton lot, in the building next to hers. Clearly, Jared had yet to move on.

Well, enough was enough. Now that she had a role in *M*A*S*H*U*P*, she wasn't going to let Jared ruin it for her. Before he could hit Calvin, she grabbed hold of her young conquest's balls and twisted them—*hard*.

He was screaming in pain as the Sunset Tower security goons grabbed him from behind and lugged him back out of the car. As the photographers' cameras flashed furiously, it dawned on her: *This is the Oscar incident everyone will be talking about tomorrow.*

Susie fashioned her face into a look of shock. Then, chest thrust forward, with one foot angled in front of the other, she began her ascent from the car.

She was already out the door when Calvin called after her, "Susie, don't! Your lipstick—honey, you look like a clown!"

Chapter 3

TALLY HAD ALREADY unloaded almost half her tray of champagne before she even made it to where her targets, Sean Penn and Johnny Depp, were standing. By then, they had crushed their cigarette stubs into the gravel and were heading inside. They barely glanced at Tally as each grabbed a flute of bubbly from the tray.

She was disappointed, but then she noticed that Johnny had left something behind: his invitation to the Governors Ball. Apparently, he had folded it so that it would fit in his jacket pocket, and when he'd pulled out his silver cigarette case (which, she'd read somewhere, had once belonged to Hunter Thompson), it had fallen out. She watched as the program flittered around in the brisk evening breeze for a few moments before a gust picked it up and blew it under the tall box hedge flanking the twenty-foot stainless-steel letters that spelled out the words *VANITY FAIR*. Although the heat lamps were on, the light wind made it feel chilly out, and everyone else began meandering back inside, too.

Perfect, she thought. *I can retrieve it without anyone seeing me.*

Tally put down her tray on a nearby table and crouched by the hedge. With one hand, she held herself steady as she probed the ground behind the shrub closest to her. She came up empty.

Damn it.

Figuring no one was around to see her, she got down on her hands and knees and crawled behind the hedge as far as she could, grasping frantically around the roots of the bushes, until she found what she was looking for.

Bingo.

She couldn't wait to add it to her other treasures. Maybe someday, when she, too, was famous and other celebrities would clamor for invitations to her dinner parties, she'd invite everyone who'd contributed to her scrapbook over and show them her collection, and they'd all have a good laugh as they reminisced about that night at the Oscar after party, and—

"Having fun?"

A man's voice interrupted her daydream. Tally froze, almost afraid to look up, figuring she was sure to get canned for acting like such an idiot.

Calm down! Just calm down. She tried to think of a way to explain herself. Finally, it came to her: *Act natural.*

She took a deep breath, set her face into a demure smile, and stood up.

She recognized the man behind the voice immediately as she came face-to-face with the sloe-eyed, chiseled-chinned Dr. Sam Jeffries from her favorite prime-time medical drama, *Intensive Care*—otherwise known as Gabriel McNamara. He was taller than he seemed on television. And blonder. And even more adorable.

When she'd first walked onto the deck, he'd been sitting by himself at one of the tables in the back corner of the garden. She'd just presumed he'd gone in, like the others, and because it was dark except for the twinkling white lights strung along the balcony, she hadn't seen him approaching as she'd pursued the fallen invitation.

Now Gabriel's slate-gray eyes moved down her body, slowly, from head to toe. If he'd had X-ray vision—and his penetrating gaze made it feel as if that might be possible—he'd have seen that her heart was racing at a million beats per minute.

He took her hand in his own, turning it palm up and revealing the engraved card. "Ah, so what do we have here?"

Tally tried to relax, but she was shaking like a leaf at his touch. "It's just a piece of paper."

"Man, the management in this place has gotten a lot stricter since I worked here. They actually make you crawl around on the ground and pick up litter?"

"What? Wait . . . you worked *here*? But—but you're Gabriel McNamara!"

"Shhh. I don't need the tabloids getting hold of that one." He put his finger to his lips. "So, you know my name, but I didn't catch yours."

"Me? Oh." *Gabriel McNamara wants to know my name!* Tally couldn't believe it. "It's Tally. Jones." She stuck out her trembling hand for him to shake.

"Nice to meet you, Tally Jones." He held on to her hand for a moment longer than he could have, as if he didn't want to let go. A warm tingle went up her spine.

Finally, he pointed back to where he'd been sitting. "Hey, I saw a trash can over there, if you want to dump that."

Reluctantly, she came out of her trance. "Oh! Um, no, that's OK. I have this." Sheepishly, she pulled out one of the plastic baggies she carried in her pockets just in case she came across a celebrity souvenir.

Later, she'd tag it with a waterproof Sharpie, scribbling the date, location, and name of the donor.

"Wait . . ." He started laughing. "Are you planning on selling that invitation on eBay or something?"

"No!" she answered, slightly embarrassed. "What do you take me for, some kind of creep?"

"Well, you do have to admit it's kind of strange to keep a random scrap of paper."

Strange. Gabriel McNamara just called me strange. Before she could help it, one tear rolled down her cheek, followed by another. She felt like a total loser.

But she wasn't a loser. She was a girl with a lot of talent and a lot of persistence.

Regaining her composure, she looked up at him. "Strange? Well, *I* don't think it's strange to keep an invitation to the Governors Ball. It's a momentous event that, as an actress, one day I would love to attend. Which is why I'm keeping this. You know, as a memento. Maybe you just think it's strange because you take all of this for granted."

There! She'd told *him* off.

Or, more accurately, turned him on. The kiss he gave her felt like an electrical charge running through her veins. Her body surged forward, as if compelled by some stronger force, to satisfy some unquenchable desire.

Slowly, he let go of her, and she remembered to breathe again.

"Consider that a memento. You know, something to remember me by, until we run into each other again. If your acting is as good as your kissing, I'm sure we will."

With the grace of a big cat, he strolled back inside the restaurant. Tally stared after him, then down at the Governors Ball invitation. Something told her that she'd remember the kiss long after the thrill of her souvenirs had worn off.

Looking back at the doorway where Gabriel had reentered the party, she barely noticed the bearded man she'd served earlier shake his head sadly before going inside.

Chapter 4

EVEN AS BONE-TIRED as Tally was the day after the *Vanity Fair* party, she knew she couldn't skip out on her acting class that night. Her teacher, the renowned drama coach Randall Littlefield, had many hard and fast rules, and rule number one was that a student could never, *ever* miss a class, even once. That meant banishment, without exception.

Another rule was that your performance had to be authentic. Otherwise, you were a phony, and Randall let you know it, in no uncertain terms—and those terms usually left you in tears, if not ready to forget your dream of being an actor altogether.

Because of their teacher's illustrious reputation in the industry, Tally, Mandy, Sadie, and Randall's other students sucked it up and stuck it out, no matter what. The serious ones, anyway. After all, rumor had it that he had once made David Duchovny cry during scene study. That story always ended with "And yet he persevered, and look where he is today!" Who could argue with that?

So, where the heck is Sadie? Tally wondered, as she glanced at the door for what felt like the hundredth time.

The two of them were to do a scene together that night. It was a well-known Meisner improv, in which Tally was to show up at Sadie's door and proclaim that she had cancer. They had worked hard on it all week, realizing that it might just be the best bit of theater they'd done all year. *Only a wreck would keep her from showing tonight,* thought Tally.

Already, Randall had announced that the class should move through their usual warm-up exercises. The students were all barefoot—which, according to Randall, kept you grounded to the earth as well as to your emotions—and positioned in a circle around their teacher as they recited a series of tongue twisters in rapid succession.

Obviously, too rapidly for Mandy. Somewhere between "Rubber baby buggy bumpers" and "Freshly fried fresh flesh," she leaned over to Tally and muttered, "It sounds like an insane asylum in here! You know, he does this just to run out the clock."

Tally nodded but kept her lips moving. She, too, had always suspected this was the case and wished they could skip the tongue twisters as well as the physical warm-up, which, had it taken place at a party, would have been called a group grope. One hundred dollars per lesson was a heck of a lot of money to spend for the privilege of babbling "mamala-mamala-papala-papala" over and over, week in and week out, and occasionally getting eviscerated by Randall for doing it wrong.

Just thinking about how much money she'd already spent this year, moving from Randall's beginner workshops to the intermediate class, made Tally lose her place in the warm-up, and she groaned out loud.

"Stop, stop!" Randall commanded, and glared over at her. "Tally, you've taken the whole class off its rhythm. Perhaps you should do 'Get Grandma' by yourself. Twenty times, please."

Great. Tally took a deep breath. "Get Grandma great Greek grapes. Get Grandma great Greek grapes. Get Grandma great Greek grapes—"

Unsatisfied, Randall interrupted her. "Your elocution! Make it *flow* trippingly off the tongue."

Tally nodded and doubled her effort to speak clearly.

Around her fourteenth "Get Grandma," she saw Sadie inching her way toward the circle from stage right. To cover for her, Tally moved in closer to Randall and, with all the precision she could muster, recited the phrase again with gusto, trying to hold Randall's attention.

Too late. Randall had seen Sadie, too. "You! Who the hell do you think you are, coming in here after class has started? If this isn't important to you, don't show up at all, because you are wasting space in my class."

Sadie blushed. "I'm so, so sorry, Randall! Traffic—"

"You bore me. Just shut up and sit down *there.*" Randall pointed toward the theater seats, in the dark abyss beyond the stage. "I'm sure you bore your class-mates, too. So that you don't waste any more of their time or mine, you'll perform last. OK, first up, some-one who won't disappoint me. Sadly, in this class, there are only a few of you . . . Erik, darling, do me proud. God, I love watching you in profile! What was your assignment? Jerry in *Betrayal?* Oh, I know you'll just be *wonderful.* Go for it—"

The air reeked of anxiety as everyone scrambled to take a seat in the audience. Tally wondered which one of them would be the first to be sacrificed on the altar of Randall's razor-sharp tongue and hoped he wouldn't save all of his venom for Sadie just out of spite.

Fortunately for Sadie, but unfortunately for everyone else, Randall tore apart *every* performance, one by one. Glancing over, Tally noticed that Mandy had chewed her nails down to the quick. Randall's tirades reached their peak as one trembling student who'd had the audacity to take on *The Vagina Monologues* struggled through her turn onstage. "Atrocious! I know Eve Ensler. Eve Ensler is a friend of mine. And *you*, Mia Antonelli, are *no* Eve Ensler! This has given me a headache. All right, students, take a five-minute break."

As a group of traumatized aspiring actors stumbled out the door to smoke, Tally nudged Sadie. "So, why were you so late to class?"

Sadie's face lit up. "Because I got a job. Full-time, and not a waitressing gig, either!"

That distracted Mandy. "Where? At the Sunset Tower?"

"No . . ." Sadie drew the word out, trying to build the suspense.

After worrying about when Sadie was going to show up for class and sitting through Randall's rants, Tally was already on her last nerve. "Sadie, if you don't just tell us what the heck you're talking about, I'm going to kill you!"

"OK." Sadie relented. "You remember how Jeff asked me to stay late and close, right? Well, I was there till, like, five in the morning, cleaning up around the booths, and guess what I found stashed under one?"

It was Mandy's turn to prod her. "We give up. Jack Nicholson?"

"No, something better." Sadie paused for dramatic effect. "Josh Gold's iPhone!"

Mandy squeaked. Of course, she and Tally knew who Josh was.

Just as Randall turned around to see who would dare make such a sound in his classroom, all three girls ducked below the row in front of them. Tally felt as if Randall's eyes were burning a hole through her. When she felt the coast was clear, she whispered, "So—what did you do with it?"

"I took it to Jeff, and he was so appreciative of my discretion that he actually let *me* return it to Josh."

"Omigod! You actually walked into *ICA*?" Mandy asked excitedly.

"Yes!" Sadie was practically glowing. "How many times have I passed that big glass office tower on Wilshire and prayed Josh Gold would step outside, right that very moment, and discover me? *Well, he did.*"

"You mean—he's going to represent you?" Tally asked.

"Well, not exactly. But right there in front of me, he fired his assistant, who had gone to the restaurant to find the phone and come back empty-handed. He told the guy he hadn't looked hard enough."

"That's too bad," Mandy said sympathetically.

"No, not really. I mean, if the dude *had* found the phone, I wouldn't have had the chance to meet Josh Gold, would I?"

Shocked, Tally leaned back in her chair. "But Sadie, the poor guy lost his job!"

"Tally, this is a tough town. It's like you said last night: we just need a little luck."

Tally shook her head. "So, what, Josh Gold was so appreciative that he just offered you the gig, right there on the spot?"

"Something like that. After he yelled at the guy to get the hell out of there, he offered me a hundred-dollar bill, as a reward. I told him to keep the cash, because I wanted the assistant job instead."

Mandy looked suspicious. "How does waiting tables qualify you to work at the ICA Agency?"

Sadie's smile faded. "It doesn't. But my degree from UCLA does. As does my typing, which is close to ninety words per minute. But what impressed Josh the most was the fact that I asked for the job."

Tally frowned. "You know, he's got a reputation for eating his assistants alive."

"We'll see about that." Sadie sat up proudly. "The three of us have spent ages struggling for even one tiny break. Well, this is mine. At ICA, I can find out how this industry works from the inside. And who knows? As my new boss gets to know me better, maybe he'll consider it an honor to represent me."

"You know we're proud of you, Sadie," Tally said, and squeezed her hand. "But be honest with yourself: those jobs are ball busters, and they don't pay very much. Is that really what you want to do?"

Sadie's smile wavered but only for a second. "Yes. I need to pay my rent—not to mention come up with the cash for these classes—and working at an agency seems as good a place as any to try to break into Hollywood." Her grin disappeared altogether. "Mandy, Randall is pointing at you. I guess you're up."

"You've inspired me, Sadie," Mandy said as she stood up. "Wish me luck."

Once onstage, Mandy looked even more rattled, but she pulled herself together as best she could and began reciting her lines. Before she could complete her second sentence in Holga's monologue from *After the Fall*, Randall stopped her short with a curt "That's enough."

Mandy looked as if she'd been slapped. "But—but I didn't get to finish."

There was a gasp in the audience. Slowly, like a cat happily eyeing a mouse, Randall looked up from his notes and said, "I beg your pardon?"

Gunshots would have sounded less menacing.

"I—I'd only just started. I didn't get to the part where—"

"Seriously, did you think I was going to sit here and let you bastardize Arthur Miller? Let me ask you a question. What made you think you were worthy even to attempt this monologue? The character is telling us how she found out that her own people—the Germans—were guilty of mass murder! You sound as if you're in Saks returning panty hose, for God's sake. I've never heard anything so aimlessly disjointed, contrived, and mediocre. At least, not to-night." He waved his hand dismissively. "Now, please don't waste another second of my time or that of your fellow students."

Mandy stood on the stage for what seemed like a lifetime. Tears rolled down both her cheeks, but she didn't bother to wipe them away. Finally, she made her way slowly off the stage. When she got down to the theater's middle aisle, she walked past her seat and continued out the door.

"And that, students, is what failure looks like," Randall said matter-of-factly. He then motioned for Tally and Sadie to take the stage. "You two are next. Unless you're as hopeless as your friend."

They exchanged shocked glances. As much as they wanted to run after Mandy and comfort her, they knew that if they followed her, they, too, could never return. And that wasn't an option if they wanted to make it in Hollywood.

Randall Littlefield loved playing God, and within the confines of his studio, he was exactly that.

Here, he wasn't over the hill or obese or stuck with a face that only his nearsighted mother ever truly loved—the same mother whose legacy had left Randall with a potato for a nose and early onset male pattern baldness.

Thank goodness he figured out early in the game that his looks and his overwrought talent weren't going to get him the fame and fortune he so desperately sought in Los Angeles, and he'd stumbled upon something that would: teaching.

Here, in the studio, where Randall had built his reputation, it didn't matter that he'd failed to make it as a working actor himself. Or, for that matter, that he was the most abusive acting teacher on either coast. In spite of all the cruelty with which he tortured his students—maybe even because of it—he was revered and fawned over.

Best of all, men who under any other circumstance wouldn't give him a second glance—handsome young studs who dreamed of being the next Brad or Denzel or Matt—hung on his every word and acted flattered when he flirted with them. And if he suggested private lessons, they never refused.

This semester, Erik was teacher's pet. Usually, he'd stay after class, under the pretense of helping Randall "tidy up the studio." Instead of cleaning up, he'd allow Randall to strip him down—literally, as opposed to figuratively—before following him to the big round bed Randall kept in his back office. There, Erik gave his best performances, on or off Randall's stage.

But not tonight.

That evening, as Randall watched Tally Jones run through her scene, he realized he had discovered a new star. *About damn time, too,* he thought. It had been too long since one of his students had hit it big. And Tally Jones was the real thing. He'd fostered her talent for the past year, and everything had finally, suddenly clicked.

The Meisner piece allowed her to burn with an intensity Randall rarely saw in an actress Tally's age. If she'd been just another pretty wannabe like the girl who went before her—that prissy little airhead Mandy—Randall would have already sliced and diced her to shreds. That was his way of getting back at all the gorgeous, seemingly vapid women— the Mandys of the world—who had rolled their eyes when Randall had shown up for auditions. But he couldn't do that to Tally Jones, because she was *just too damn good.* She really had something: star quality, like a Meryl or a Cate, along with a vulnerability that made it possible for her actually to inhabit a character.

Certainly, Randall himself had never shone like that onstage. But that was OK with him; if Tally hit it out of the park, Randall would be right there at her side, because the young stars don't truly believe their luck. They worry that they don't deserve it, so they look for a crutch. *I'll be her crutch, and her success will just reinforce my place in the Hollywood food chain.*

When Tally and her friend were done with their scene, Randall actually stood up and walked toward the stage. Lifting both his hands toward Tally, he declared, "Excellent!"

The other students in the audience murmured their relief.

Then Randall glanced over at Sadie, who was still holding her breath. "You, on the other hand, were a disappointment. She told you she had cancer, and what did you do? It looked as if you were *yawning*. Don't you have any real emotions that you can draw upon? You do? Well, surprise, surprise. Why did you keep them to yourself, where they do absolutely no good? Sometimes I don't even know why people like you show up to class. You're dismissed."

He turned back to Tally and gave her a grand smile.

"Tally, dear, do you have a moment to talk to me after class? There is a very special monologue I'd like you to work on for next week. I think it fits you perfectly. You may very well be master class material, and this scene might give you a chance to prove it."

Chapter 5

ONCE THE PAPERWORK had been signed for her to star in *M*A*S*H*U*P*, Susie Sheppard's publicist put out a press release proclaiming her the new Hot Lips Houlihan. Everyone on the Hollywood beat—from *Variety* and *Entertainment Weekly* and Page Six to *The Hollywood Reporter* and *People*—was in shock. E! Online's Ted Casablanca even blogged about it as a "Blind Vice" item, inferring that Calvin had lost his head (and he'd pretty much spelled out which head he was referring to). Perez Hilton, on the other hand, had his fans write in with names of actresses they'd prefer to see in the role. The list ran twenty-three names long.

No one wrote in to defend Susie. Except, of course,

for her publicist. Unfortunately, the ninny had forgotten to use one of the many fake e-mail accounts she'd created for just this kind of client backlash, and Perez pointed that out, too. (Susie's new publicist swore on her own mother's grave that would *never* happen at her shop, since their social networking was outsourced to a firm in China.)

Susie knew that none of this really mattered. She had Calvin in the palm of her hand (and in her mouth, on most evenings), and no one—especially not some bitchy blogger—could trump that. But when Calvin broke the news to her that the weather in Egypt, which was going to stand in for Iraq as the shooting location, was better during the months she was in production with *Dana Point*, and therefore she might have a scheduling conflict, Susie knew she had a problem. She had to get out of her contract with *Dana Point*, at any cost.

Her new publicist immediately started doing her bit. The latest cover of *People* heralded the fight between Susie and Burt Tillman, the producer of *Dana Point*, with the headline "Off *Point:* Susie Sheppard Wants Out, and Here's Why." The accompanying article vilified Burt for holding her back from her true destiny, playing "the most dynamic Hot Lips Houlihan audiences have ever seen." It then went on to document in photos (for the print edition) and video clips (for the online version) the memorable Susie-isms that made *Dana Point* such an addictive show.

A private tea for two at Susie's cozy abode had given the *People* reporter just the right perspective on this egregious studio power grab.

"Being on set is torture! Not to mention the torturous interference with my career. I have no recourse but to sue Mr. Tillman," Susie was quoted as saying. Through a veil of tears, she'd added, "And besides, it's the break of a lifetime! Why would he be so mean? The show's ratings have been slipping for so long I feel as if I'm on the *Titanic*." To drive her point home, Susie had spread her arms apart and leaned forward, as if she were Kate Winslet in the movie that made her career.

The reporter had fallen for it, hook, line, and sinker.

Burt Tillman knew better. Susie had positioned herself that way to ensure that the photographer got a great angle on her tits. He said as much to Susie's agent, Josh Gold, who'd shown up in Burt's palatial offices in the grand tower on the Royalton lot to plead her case. It was three o'clock—or, in Burt Tillman's world, happy hour. Every weekday afternoon at that time, he downed an entire bottle of scotch as he watched that morning's dailies for *Dana Point* in the office screening room.

"So, Susie wants to sue me? Ha! I'd like to see that conniving, no-talent tart try. Contractually, she's got another four years on the show, and it's ironclad. Tell her to go fuck herself."

Josh nodded benignly. He'd threatened bloody hell first, staying the course with Susie's hard line, but he was a realist and knew Susie's best acting was done between the sheets. Hell, that's how she'd gotten him to represent her in the first place. Now he was trying to play good cop.

"Listen, Burt," Josh said plaintively. "Maybe we can work this out. I mean, who knows if Susie's movie career will even pan out."

It was a good point but not good enough, in Burt's opinion. "What am I supposed to do, wait for her movie career to implode and pray that she comes back with her tail between her legs? Bullshit." As she flickered on the screen in front of him, Burt raised his scotch and soda to her, then turned to Josh. "Listen. If it were up to me, I'd say to hell with her. But the viewers love her cold-fish routine. If only they knew it wasn't acting."

At this, Josh nodded almost imperceptibly.

"Look, Josh, bottom line: I'm not folding on this. So man up and tell her that if she breaches her contract, she'll be wrapped up in one ugly lawsuit for a long time. Not only that, no one will dare hire her—not even that dickhead director Calvin, who she's been blowing. And SAG certainly won't protect her in a fight against me."

Josh swallowed hard. His next stop was Susie's trailer, where he'd have to break the news to her that Burt wasn't about to bend. He downed the last drop of scotch from his glass and walked out.

The only time Susie ever picked up the tab was when she was out drinking with her old pal, Rosanna. And that was only because Rosanna had too much dirt on her. Otherwise, she'd just be another sick, sorry memory from Susie's past.

Not that all of Susie's memories of Rosanna were bad. Back in the day, they had both worked at the same escort service, and they were often paired for girl-on-girl action, which both of them had enjoyed greatly. On particularly interesting nights, clients would ask to watch some BDSM between the two of them. That was fine with Susie, because Rosanna never minded being the submissive. Susie fondly recalled the way Rosanna squealed with pain when she'd taken a cat-o-nine-tails to her big, voluptuous ass. Those were the days . . .

Usually, Susie insisted that they meet at some dive bar in the Valley, but during their last meeting, Rosanna had called her out. "I'm beginning to think you don't want people to see us together in public," she'd whined menacingly.

Susie took the hint, and that evening, they were tucked into one of the alcoves at the Chateau Marmont. It was trendy enough to appease Rosanna, but their poorly lit little nook gave Susie some cover. Plus, Susie hoped that she might be able to talk Rosanna into giving her a freebie later. In anticipation, she'd already rented one of the hillside bungalows and made sure that Rosanna drank expansively and expensively. Tonight she was plying her girlfriend with Chivas Regal, which usually made Rosanna very chatty. She had a big mouth and loved to name-drop, which was just fine with Susie, who always took note of the who-where-when-and-what-position info Rosanna provided, then traded the salacious tidbits with her favorite gossip gadflies for reprieves on her own bad behavior.

Unfortunately, Rosanna had picked tonight of all nights to play coy. "I'm through kissing and telling. It's bad for business," she said, her words slurring together. The Chivas hit both her brain and her bladder at the same time. "I'll be right back," she muttered as she slipped off the sofa and stumbled to the bathroom.

Susie would not have even noticed that Rosanna had left her purse if her old pal's cell phone hadn't started to buzz. *Aha*, she thought. *Let's see who the lucky boy is tonight . . .*

Susie reached over and opened the purse. Fumbling inside, she found the phone and pulled it out. She snickered when she saw Rosanna actually listed her johns' real names in her contacts. In fact, her phone was currently flashing the name of a well-known sitcom star who was notorious for his fondness for hookers.

Susie yawned. No big surprise there.

She started flipping through the contacts, which Rosanna listed by first name and last initial, followed by the person's favorite sex act. By the time she reached the B's, she'd found what she was looking for:

Burt T—Dom.

But of course. Despite his having built her a fifty-three-room castle atop the fabulous LA enclave of Bel Air, Burt's old battle-ax of a wife, Babs, could barely stand living with the old drunk, let alone lower herself to have sex with him—or whatever else he liked to do, which, according to Rosanna's code, involved a little pain.

Great, Susie figured. Because tonight he was going to get royally fucked. And she was going to get out of her contract.

She was still looking down at the answer to her troubles when she heard Rosanna's voice behind her. "Hey, that's my phone!"

"Well, it was ringing. Don't worry, I didn't answer it," Susie said, and tossed the phone at her.

Rosanna fumbled the catch. She might have freshened up, but she couldn't hide the fact that she was still three sheets to the wind as she checked her messages. "Aw, damn it! Just had a cancellation," she said with a frown.

"Oh, well, tell you what. Why don't I make good on it?" Susie smiled knowingly at Rosanna, who licked her lips.

"Sure! What do you have in mind?"

"Believe it or not, I'm in the mood to watch."

Rosanna giggled. "Nothing like the old days, huh? OK, let me call Carlotta to see if she's around—"

"Hell, no, I don't mean you and some other bitch. How about you and one of your johns? They won't even know I'm there."

Rosanna shrugged. "Sure, whatever. I've got an up-and-coming actor dude who loves to—"

"No, it's my dime, so I get to choose the lucky boy," Susie interrupted as she snatched the phone out of her friend's hand. She scrolled through the B's until she got to Burt's name, then handed the phone back to her friend. "And I choose *him*."

Rosanna wrinkled her nose. "Ick! This will set you back, like, a grand."

"You just doubled your rate on me, you whore!"

"When he gets here, you'll see why." Rosanna shuddered but hit "send" anyway. "Hello, handsome! It's your mama! I'm guessin' baby boy has been very, very bad today, and I've got a deal you can't refuse. I'm at the Marmont, and a client just canceled on me, but the room is paid for, and I'm *so* lonely. . . . Yeah, I'm being serious! Let's call this an early birthday present. I brought my cuffs and that bad-boy paddle you love—you know, the leather one with the studs. Half an hour? Yep, just go up to hillside bungalow number three. See ya then."

Susie waited until Burt was bound and gagged before entering the bedroom. Rosanna had done just as she'd been asked: gotten naked and handcuffed him to the bedposts. He was on his knees, and he groaned when he saw Susie, who was trussed up in Rosanna's dominatrix catsuit. When she picked up his cell phone, he almost choked on his gag.

Susie just laughed. "Are you ready for your close-up?" Without waiting for him to nod, shake his head, or cry, she started clicking away. Then she snapped her fingers at Rosanna. "Get over there, and do your thing."

Rosanna nodded, then positioned herself beside Burt and gave him a light swat—then another, even harder, then again, and again—and she didn't stop until the tears were streaming down his face and his scorched backside was streaked with red welts. Every time she hit him, her large naked breasts swung back and forth, like twin pendulums.

Under different circumstances, Susie would have been turned on, but not tonight. Too much was at stake.

"I think he's going to have a heart attack," Rosanna muttered as Burt gasped for air. Susie's look told her it was time to get lost, and Rosanna complied. Not even stopping to get dressed, she grabbed her clothes and skedaddled out of the cottage.

When Burt finally calmed down, Susie sat down beside him on the bed. "Between you and me, Burt, your little thing for Rosanna's paddle is nothing. However, I'm guessing it's something you're keeping from Babs and the kids, and things might get ugly for you if she got a hold of these little snapshots. Am I right?" She stroked the cell phone lovingly. "I'm also guessing the two of us can resolve our little disagreement to everyone's satisfaction. But let me assure you: if, for any reason, we don't see eye-to-eye, Babs will see the photos. They'll also be delivered to every studio executive in town, not to mention the tabloids."

He started sniveling, and she knew she had him.

She took the gag out of his mouth and said soothingly, "Burt, darling, all of this goes away the minute you agree to let me out of my contract. So, what do you say?"

"Yes! *Yes!*"

She released him from the handcuffs and tossed him the cell phone. He started deleting the images as fast as his trembling fingers would let him.

As she walked out of the room, she waved goodbye. She didn't bother to tell him that she'd already e-mailed the images to herself. She didn't have to. She'd lived in Hollywood long enough to know that it was always good to have an insurance policy, and he'd worked with her long enough to know that she'd try to hold the photos over him for the rest of his career.

Chapter 6

THE GIRL RUNNING on the treadmill in front of him was long-legged and lithe, with a firm, pert ass. In other words, Steve Fisher's type.

He'd been dumped by his latest protégée, which had hurt, but Steve knew the score. Women didn't date him for his looks. For God's sake, he was over fifty, balding (despite the ponytail), and much too gaunt for his string bean–thin frame: at six-feet four inches, he tipped the scales at only one hundred and fifty-five pounds.

Despite the fact that he was a hotshot talent manager, once Steve put the girls of his dreams on the path to stardom, inevitably they left him for someone else. He was always being replaced by someone more powerful and prominent, and to add insult to injury, more often than not, he'd made the introduction.

The fact that the women moved on the moment they got any kind of traction in their careers had taught him a lesson: If he wanted to hang on to them, he had to keep them close and try not to let them become too famous too soon. Of course, he wanted them to be successful—after all, that's how he made his living—but the less secure they felt, the more they depended on Steve, and he loved the role of Svengali. So, occasionally, he "forgot" to send his starlets out on auditions. When they wondered why they weren't being considered for a part, he'd comfort them, and they'd feel more reliant on him than ever.

To get a better look at the treadmill cutie, Steve moved over to the empty machine to her right. From that angle, he could get a close-up of her face in the mirror in front of them. What he noticed first were those beautiful, large, hazel eyes. Then he saw that she was reading a copy of *The Hollywood Reporter*.

Ah, an actress. Well, this was certainly going to be easy . . .

"I don't remember seeing you before. Are you new here?"

Tally looked up from her *THR*, slightly annoyed.

The man had been staring at her from the back of the room for the past twenty minutes, and as if being creepy weren't enough, now he was interfering with her workout. But her annoyance faded immediately when she realized who was bothering her.

It was Steve Fisher.

She knew she shouldn't be surprised to see him there. After all, one of the reasons she'd joined that specific gym was that it was right in the heart of Beverly Hills, and she'd heard a lot of Hollywood players were members. Networking was networking, even if you were spandex-clad and sweaty, right?

Steve Fisher was pretty high up on the list of players she wanted to meet. He managed the careers of a lot of up-and-coming stars, and he'd dated many of her favorite starlets. She'd seen photos of him in *Vanity Fair* and *People* with various young actresses on his arm; most recently, he'd been snapped on the red carpet at the Golden Globes with a British actress who had done a lot of PBS costume dramas and was now trying to pick up some American films.

Tally slowed down the pace of her treadmill. Her dimple deepened as she smiled. "I only joined last week."

He looked down at her magazine, as if noticing it for the first time, then looked directly into her eyes and said, "You must be an actress." When she nodded, he smiled appreciatively. "What would I have seen you in?"

That wiped the smile off her face. "Nothing . . . yet. But I'm studying with Randall Littlefield. In fact, he's just invited me to join his master class."

"Randall? He's the best! Even after actors make it, they're always working on their craft, and they surround themselves with good people like Randall." He punched the setting of his treadmill to a crawl. "Do you mind me asking if you've got a manager yet?"

"A manager? *Me?*" Tally's eyes widened. "No, not yet . . ."

He held out his hand. "I'm Steve Fisher. That's what I do."

Looking slightly embarrassed as she took it, she said, "To tell you the truth, I already know who you are."

Steve smiled. *This is going to be easier than I thought . . .*

"Tally, you look like a million dollars."

The look in Steve's eyes made Tally blush, but when she looked at herself in the mirror, she had to agree.

Then again, the dress was Gucci; while not exactly a million dollars, it might as well have been, considering her budget.

It had been a week since Steve had offered to represent her. She had hesitated at first, because she couldn't believe her luck. But with both Sadie and Mandy insisting that she take him up on it, she'd finally called his office and stammered out a promise to work hard and never to let him down. In turn, he had made it clear to her that while he had no issues with her talent, she didn't look the part of a star. "If you're going to make it in this town, you've got to look like you belong here," he said.

The dress certainly accomplished that. It was black, strapless, and slinky. The fact that it hugged her tightly all over made her self-conscious. "Gosh, I can barely walk in this," she murmured.

"That's OK, nobody walks in LA anyway. All you have to do is stand and smile while the paps snap your picture. Remember, the goal is to have people talk about you and wonder who you are. We've got to put you out there, make you visible. How do you think Kim Kardashian got started, or Paris Hilton? Trust me, those ladies have nothing on you, doll."

Except money, thought Tally.

"I hear you, Steve. But—well, I just want to say up front that those aren't exactly my role models. I was hoping we'd position me as the next Reese Witherspoon or maybe Anne Hathaway."

Steve shrugged. "Yeah, sure, OK. Here, put these

on." He handed her a pair of six-inch stiletto heels. Then, noting the slim, low-slung jeans on a mannequin, he motioned to the Gucci shop girl. "Bring over a pair of those in her size. She'll also need a couple of those tops, there." He pointed to a rack of sheer, glittery blouses. "And those sunglasses. Oh, yeah, and a bikini, too. I like that silvery one. What do you think, Tally?"

When Tally looked at the price tag, she nearly fainted. "Steve, I can't afford this! Really, I don't make nearly enough money to buy *any* of this. I'm just a waitress, remember?"

"Sweetheart, you can't afford *not* to invest in your wardrobe. Not to mention your face and your hair. Thank God you've already got a great body. Otherwise, I'd have to set you up with my nip/tuck guy, too."

Seeing the shocked look on her face, he gave her a hug—and held on to her for a little too long.

"Look, let's just make this an advance on your future earnings. After you get a few roles under your belt, I'll deduct what you owe me. You know, a little at a time, here and there."

"Well, OK." Tally exhaled—or at least tried to. The dress barely gave her any room to breathe.

Gucci was only their first stop on Rodeo Drive. Steve also wanted to take her to Dolce & Gabbana and Prada. Then they'd meander toward Melrose, hitting

Madison, Diavolina, and Fred Segal on the way—none of which she'd ever dare to enter on her own. But now that she was represented by Steve Fisher, she belonged in these places. At least, Steve thought so. And who was she to argue with him? Besides, no man had ever taken such an interest in her. And she had to admit it: she looked stunning in the body-hugging clothing he picked out.

Apparently, others thought so, too, as evidenced by the many admiring he glances she got that evening as she and Steve roamed from one see-and-be-seen spot to another. They began with dinner at Madeo, where Tally picked at her salad while she stared at the stars who glittered all around her. Courteney Cox and David Arquette sat at the table beside them, while Gwen Stefani ate demurely across the room. And wasn't that Posh and David Beckham in the back booth? She felt as if she were in a dream. But no, she was really there, *living* her dream. And someday, when she was a big star, too, these very celebrities would wave at her and invite her to sit with them. *Someday soon*, she vowed to herself.

Tally was disappointed to see that Steve was more interested in the food than in the company. By the way he wolfed down his spaghetti Bolognese, Tally wondered how he stayed so thin.

From Madeo, they went for drinks at the Tower Bar

and afterward sat poolside in one of the Viceroy's cabanas before ending the night at the Polo Lounge at
the Beverly Hills Hotel, where Steve's favorite table
sat smack dab in the center of a galaxy of stars. Steve
might not have been managing Nicole Kidman or
Brad Pitt, but he certainly garnered their nods, waves,
and handshakes, and Tally soaked it all in.

Everywhere they went, Tally made sure she
grabbed a few matchbooks. When she found herself in
the ladies' room at the Polo Lounge with Renée Zellweger, she tried hard not to stare as the star reapplied
gloss to her lips, then stopped, looking at the MAC
tube in frustration. "Oh, no! It just ran out," Renée
murmured to herself. She glanced over to Tally. "Don't
you hate it when that happens?" Tally just smiled and
nodded, too starstruck to respond. Resigned to her
plight, Renée sighed, then smacked her lips to even
out what little gloss had been applied before tossing
the empty tube into the trash basket and heading out
the door.

Tally waited until she heard the *clack* of the celebrated actress's heels fade before plucking the tube
out of the basket. It would make a great addition to her
star memorabilia collection.

Then it struck her. Had she actually said something to Renée, the memory of their conversation
would have been the best keepsake of all.

Steve is only partially right, she thought. *It's not enough that I have to look as if I belong here in Hollywood. I have to act as if I belong, too.*

Tally looked down at the lip gloss in her hand. Even as she placed it in her purse, she knew it would be her very last celebrity souvenir.

Steve had just motioned the waiter for the bill when she got to the table. "Hey, what took you so long? Renée Zellweger just stopped by. If you'd been here, I could have introduced you to her." Seeing Tally's eyes grow wide, he laughed. "No big deal. There's always next time, right? Speaking of next time, why don't we hit Malibu tomorrow night? Renée mentioned some shindig at Katzenberg's. Wear that low-cut dress from Fred Segal."

Tally couldn't wait.

And so it went, from that night forward. As Steve explained it, the game plan was to get "out there" as much as possible, to see and be seen by the town's movers, shakers, and hipsters.

It was fun, but she felt odd having him as her date. He was perhaps twenty-five years older than she, maybe more, but she really couldn't tell, because his forehead had no wrinkles, and he colored what was left of his hair an auburn hue. But the hairs on his chest were gray—she knew this because the top two buttons of his shirt were always undone.

Granted, she was very appreciative of all he was doing for her. But on those nights he took her out on the town—say, to one of the many nonprofit benefits that were packed solid with B- and C-list celebrities— he acted so proprietary. If she were to be honest with herself, she'd have to admit that he acted as if she *belonged* to him.

For example, if someone attempted to talk to her—and especially if that someone just so happened to be male, younger than Steve, or handsome—Steve would interrupt or pull her away with some ridiculous excuse.

She couldn't understand why. "Steve, don't you know who that was? He's the director of that new HBO hit show, and he says there's a part coming up that might be perfect for me—"

"Bull. If there were, I'd send you up for it, you know that. Tally, baby, you've got to trust me on this: he's just trying to get into your pants."

It was on the tip of her tongue to say, *Like you?* But she thought better of it. Of course, he was looking out for her best interests. After all, he was her manager.

Still, that didn't make it any less creepy when he put his hands on her. And there was always a hand of his *somewhere*. She didn't mind when he steered her through a crowd by the elbow, but it made her shiver when he put a hand on the small of her back or when he absentmindedly patted her ass. Or, worse yet, when he tried to kiss her good night. She avoided it by giggling and quickly slipping out of the car or by coughing and claiming she was coming down with a cold, but she knew she couldn't keep up these little games forever.

She just prayed he'd get her a job before then.

Chapter 7

DUNNO. SHE'S NOT what we have in mind, is she? I think she's too short," the network suit said to the sitcom's show runner, as if Tally wasn't standing a mere seven feet away. "Whattaya think?"

Nonchalantly, Tally tried to make herself look taller by straightening her shoulders and tossing her head back as the assistant who was reading with her paused in the middle of a line for the verdict from her boss. The show runner kept them all waiting a full two minutes while he finished texting, then finally he looked up and squinted at Tally. "Nah, I'm not so worried about her height. The read was decent, I guess, but I'm more concerned that she looks *too* fresh. You know, our lead is a bit more—well, sea-soned."

Too fresh. What the heck did *that* mean? Apparently, it meant *adios,* and don't let the door hit you on the way out.

Despite Steve's reluctance to push her too hard (his excuse), Tally cajoled a steady number of auditions out of him. The good news was that she was making the rounds. The bad news was that by now, she'd heard every possible turndown. From the get-go, the process was disheartening. Tally was undoubtedly talented, but so were many of the women in the reception room waiting to try out for a part, not to mention those who made up the line that flowed out the door.

And if the producers and directors weren't whispering throughout her audition, they were talking loudly on their cell phones or (like the show runner who apparently was looking for someone not so "fresh") texting as opposed to paying attention.

Callbacks could be just as brutal. And because she was such a "fresh face," Tally sometimes got called back three or four times, only to be told that she was too young, too old, too short, too tall, not pretty enough, or too pretty. Sometimes they simply said, "It's not going to work out this time," or worse yet, "We're no longer going forward with this project." Bottom line: no work for Tally.

She knew for certain that was the case this time, too, when the casting director smiled up at her brightly, then gave her the ultimate generic let-down: "Sorry, hon, but we're going in another direction."

How many times had she heard that one? She shrugged, grabbed her purse, and stumbled out the door.

The tears were streaming down her face by the time she reached her car. Still too upset to drive, she checked her makeup in the rearview mirror. Seeing her face there, she went into character: the character the show runner would have *loved* had he only taken the time to listen to her say her lines, as she was saying them now.

Screw him, she thought. With the hurt and anger out of her system, still looking in the mirror, she set her lips into a smile. After six weeks, she and Sadie were finally going to see Mandy, and the last thing her sensitive friend needed was to see her crying.

Tally and Sadie were anxious to see her. For the first two weeks after Mandy had left Randall's class, neither of them had been able to get her to answer her phone or even respond to a text message. Camping out on the doorstep of her studio apartment hadn't worked, either. When they came by, she either pretended she wasn't home or pleaded with them to leave her alone. "Seriously, I'm OK," she said. "I just don't feel great about myself right now. Please, just give me a little more breathing room."

Finally, that morning, Mandy had responded positively to Sadie's threat to break down the door with a crowbar. "Oh, OK! But I've got to warn you: I've been doing a lot of thinking—among other things. In fact, I have something to show you. It puts my career in a different perspective."

That was all they needed to hear to feel some relief. At least Mandy still felt she *had* a career.

They'd decided to meet at the Denny's on Sunset, where they had always gotten together for cheap food and gossip in the old days—those days being close to six weeks ago, before Tally had Steve in her life and Sadie began working for Josh.

By the time Tally got there, the restaurant was just filling up with the early dinner patrons. Sadie had arrived first and snagged the back corner booth. She patted the seat beside her as Tally approached. "Well, how did it go?"

"Badly. I feel like such a loser." Tally still had the smile on her face, but she could feel it quivering.

Sadie noticed. "The last thing you are is a loser, and you know it. Just look at how much you've accomplished in a few short weeks. You actually have a manager! Plus, you've been promoted to Randall's master class."

Tally caught the edge in Sadie's voice. With her advancement and Mandy quitting the class, Sadie had to fend for herself in Randall's intermediate course. She glanced up anxiously at her friend. "You don't hate me, do you?"

"Of course not! I just wish it were *me* as opposed to you who was getting rejected at all those auditions." She frowned as she pushed away her water glass. "Then again, maybe not. I guess what I'm trying to say is that it would be nice to have the opportunity to audition, even if nothing came of it. Right now, with as hard as Josh is working me, I might never have an acting career."

"Why do you say that? Sadie, you're meeting so many new people! Directors, screenwriters, stars, casting directors—"

"Big deal! They don't see me as an actress. They see me as Josh's gofer who brings them coffee and jumps like a puppet whenever he throws a screaming fit." She rolled her eyes at the thought. "And that's every hour on the hour. I should know, because he expects me at my desk by eight every morning, and sometimes I don't leave until nine o'clock. And if there is some event that he or his clients need me to attend with them, I might not get home until after midnight. I had to lie and say I had a doctor's appointment just so I could leave to come here."

"I had no idea. I guess we've both been so busy we haven't caught up in a while," Tally said as she took a sip of her water. "So, are you going to quit?"

"I don't know. Well, I guess not yet." Sadie grabbed a roll from the free bread basket their waitress had brought over and spread butter on half. "You want to hear something funny? I've got no one to blame but myself. I'm actually pretty good at what I do. It's almost as if I can read Josh's mind. And to tell you the truth, as frustrated as I am about having to put my acting on hold, I don't mind working late with him."

Tally smiled. "Just what's that supposed to mean?"

"You've got to admit it, he is sort of cute. I mean, if you like immature guys who curse you out one minute, then tell you how he'd be lost without you the next." Sadie shrugged. "He might be right about that. My God, I truly believe that if I were a guy, he'd make me follow him into the john and wipe his butt for him."

"No wonder you don't have time to go to auditions."

"I might be dropping out of class, too. Last week, I was late again and got railed on by Randall." Sadie grimaced as she said this. "Besides, class isn't fun anymore without you or Mandy there, sweating it out with me."

"Speaking of Mandy, what do you think is her big surprise?"

Sadie, who had been periodically glancing at the entrance to the Denny's, choked on her water. "She's wearing it! Or I should say, it's wearing *her*."

Tally looked up to see Mandy walking toward them. She wasn't the only one. Mandy now had the attention of every man in the room—38D's on a tiny frame like Mandy's were certainly eye openers, and the top she was wearing definitely added to the effect. It was tight and sheer enough to make out her nipples, which, despite the obvious fact that she wasn't wearing a bra, were firm and high.

Ignoring the stares, she sauntered slowly to the table and slid into the booth. "So, what do you think?"

Tally gulped. "I'm going to go out on a limb and predict that you'll at least get a reading from any director you meet. How about you, Sadie?" Tally waited for her friend to agree. When Sadie didn't speak up, Tally nudged her. "She's not Medusa, Sadie. You didn't turn to stone."

Sadie blinked twice, then exhaled. "Mandy . . . *why*?"

Mandy sighed. "Sadie, let's face it: Randall was right. I don't have half the talent you and Tally have. And I guess I just got tired of casting directors looking in every direction but mine. Now they'll look right at me." She pushed her shoulders back and proudly looked around the room. "Like every other man. And you know what? I *love* it!"

Tally frowned. "Randall is just trying to toughen us up for the audition process."

"No," Sadie said slowly, and took another sip of her water. "Randall is unnecessarily vicious. He should be inspiring us to greater heights, not driving us to desperation." She gave Mandy's breasts a sidelong glance. "They're double D's, right? Aren't they heavy?"

"OK, yeah, maybe I went a *bit* overboard. Even the doctor was a little concerned," Mandy said, sheepish.

Tally shook her head. "If he was concerned, why didn't you listen to him? Look, Mandy, I know you weren't happy with what you had, but now you could get a job in the Playboy Mansion."

Mandy giggled uneasily. "Hey, don't think I haven't thought about it! I used all of my savings and part of my rent money to pay for the girls here. If I can't come up with five hundred bucks in the next week, I'll be kicked out of my apartment."

"If you need a place to crash, you know you can always sleep on my couch," Tally said as she reached over to give Mandy a hug.

"That's sweet of you, but I don't know if there will

be room for me and the twins on your couch. These babies take up a lot of space, if you haven't noticed."

"Trust me, we have. And so has every guy in this room," Sadie said as she dabbed her lips with a napkin. "Hey, you can move in with me, if you want. My roomie's moving out at the end of the month. And thanks to work, I'm barely there anymore, so you'll have lots of privacy."

"Sadie, thank you!" Mandy looked as if she was about to cry. Then, glancing over her shoulder, she muttered, "Oh my God, that guy is actually coming over here."

Sadie guffawed. "Something tells me he won't be the last. You've now got a natural homing device for jerks. You'd better get used to it."

The jerk in question was short—not even five-foot-seven—but he had wide sculpted shoulders and, from what the girls could make out through his tight T-shirt, massive biceps and an admirable six-pack. His red hair was scruffy, as was his goatee, and he certainly had an air of confidence about him.

When he reached the table, he ignored Sadie and Tally and focused exclusively on Mandy. "Hey, you're not an actress, are you?"

"As a matter of fact, I am," Mandy replied primly. "And by the way, so are my friends here."

He barely nodded at the other two girls, then gave

Mandy a business card. "Here, take this, OK? We're always looking for extras."

Mandy scrutinized it. "Dandy Candy Productions? What do you make, kiddie films?"

The man snickered. "Not exactly. There's not a lot of dialogue. It's just a whole bunch of girls and boys having fun. *Lots* of fun, if you catch my drift."

"You mean you do comedies?" Mandy asked, excited. "I've always wanted to do comedy. I'm classically trained, and most of my stage work has been dramas—"

The guy cut her short with a hearty laugh, then he winked at her. "We pride ourselves on how expressive our actresses are, and we totally appreciate improv. Why don't you come over sometime tomorrow and check us out? I'm sure we can put you in a scene or two. We shoot in the late afternoon."

"Wow! Sure, but . . . are you a SAG signatory? Because I'm not in the union yet. How much does it pay?"

The man brushed off her concerns with a shrug. "Don't worry about SAG, and yeah, the money is great—if you're as good as you look." His grin said it all: he thought she'd be great.

Mandy smiled back seductively. "OK, yeah, sure." She followed him with her eyes as he walked away.

"Give me that card," Sadie demanded. Mandy handed it to her, and Sadie looked at the address.

"You know, this is all the way out in the Valley. In Chatsworth. *Omigod!*"

"What's the matter?" Tally took the card. After reading it, she looked up sharply at Mandy. "That guy—Jerry Conover—he produces porn!"

"What?" Mandy grabbed the card back. "How do you know that?"

Sadie pulled out a new iPhone from her purse.

"Wow," Tally said. "When did you get that?"

"It's from ICA, in case Josh needs to reach me or I need to look something up when I'm out of the office at a meeting." She fiddled with the phone for a second, then showed her friends the screen. "See? According to Google, Dandy Candy makes films with titles like *Hot and Bothered, Mother May I*, and *Prince Cumalot*. I'm guessing none of them has been up for an Oscar."

"Oh . . . no," Mandy said, tearing up. "I just can't catch a break."

Tally knocked her water glass with Mandy's. "Hey, you and me both."

Sadie suddenly sat up straight. "I just had an idea! Josh can't figure out how on earth she did it, but Susie Sheppard was able to break her contract with Burt Tillman, and he's looking for a replacement for her on *Dana Point*. Apparently, they want a 'fresh face.' You're both certainly fresh! Why not audition for it?"

Mandy frowned. "That's easy for Tally, she has a manager who'll get her in. But what am I supposed to do, just crash the audition?"

"I can set it up for you. That is, *Josh* can. And since all his calls go through me, if any questions come up, I'll make sure you're cleared."

Mandy shook her head uncertainly. "But what if he finds out? Won't he fire you?"

"They'll only call if they want you back for a second audition or if they want to offer you the role. If that happens, then Josh will certainly be happy to represent you, and it'll be a feather in my cap, too, because I discovered you for him." She smiled proudly. "It's a win-win all around."

"Will you vouch for me, too?" Tally asked softly.

Her friends turned to her. "Don't you think Steve will send you up for it?" Sadie asked.

Tally shook her head. "He must have heard they're looking, but for whatever reason, he hasn't mentioned it to me. Since that's the case, I'd rather he didn't know—at least, not unless something comes out of the audition." It was hard for her to tell them the truth: that she suspected he might actually be afraid she'd succeed and then leave him.

Mandy looked confused. "But if you get it, won't he be angry that he didn't get the commission?"

"He might be angry, but it won't be about that."

Tally sounded resolute. "Not that it matters. Besides, he'll still be my manager, so he'll get his cut. What do you say, Sadie?"

"Sure, whatever you want." Sadie raised her water glass for a toast. "Here's to one of you landing on the show. Can you imagine being able to say, 'I took Susie Sheppard's place on *Dana Point*'?"

Chapter 8

"THEY'RE READY FOR you now." The receptionist for Burt Tillman Productions nodded toward a set of double doors at the end of the hallway.

Don't panic, Tally thought. *You can do this.*

She didn't jog quickly down the hall like the girl before her had done, only to sprint back out a minute later with tears in her eyes. Instead, Tally walked slowly and steadily and tried not to get distracted by the posters of all the hit shows that lined both sides of the corridor.

Before she turned the knob, she closed her eyes, took a deep breath, and vowed, "I will get this role."

There were six people in the room. She didn't recognize the director, Larry Hornsby, and the show runner, Chase Bracken, but she knew who Burt Tillman was.

The casting director beckoned her to the front of the room. Sadie had made sure that both Mandy and Tally received the scene pages in advance, and Tally had spent the night before memorizing her lines and playing them out, again and again, in front of her mirror at home.

But her plan wasn't just to read the lines and pray that they chose her. She wanted fully to embody the character, Jamie, a bright, single woman who had grown up in Dana Point but whose family had moved away when she was a young girl because of some scandal that wouldn't be revealed until later in the season. Her love interest was to be the character Hank Franklin, a real estate developer whose fiancée, Katherine, the character that had been played by Susie Sheppard, was now in a coma. This would leave him with a dilemma. Would he stay loyal to a woman who was more than likely brain-dead or rediscover the love he had for his childhood sweetheart?

Tally meticulously prepared for the role. First, she watched the most recent season's episodes online in order to familiarize herself with the plotlines and characters and to get a feel for the program's directorial tone. Jamie was supposed to be an excellent sailor, and for the audition, Tally had bought an outfit that fit the profile: white jeans, a blue-and-white-striped boatneck top, and Sperry Top-Siders. Just dressing for the part put her in a different frame of mind. She wouldn't have much time to make an impression; just three small scenes.

Utilizing the techniques she'd learned in Randall's class—digging deep into her emotions and keeping it authentic—she'd gone over the audition scene again and again, acting it out in a variety of ways. Finally, she'd settled on what she thought was the best possible way to play it. Tally knew she had to be convincing as Jamie, whose innocence is shattered in the scene when she hears that the one man she's been pining for not only is about to be married to another woman—a woman now in a coma, at that—but also was the cause of her father's financial ruin. Much of Tally's emotion would have to be expressed in her eyes, through a tremor in her voice, and with a flinch she'd practiced, and she was ready to reflect the devastation Jamie feels at hearing about Hank's dual betrayal.

Well, it's now or never, Tally thought.

Burt Tillman's rage over Susie's blackmailing stunt had not yet subsided. After stumbling out of the hotel like a prisoner who had just been given a reprieve, he went through a series of emotions: disbelief, denial, outrage . . . but not acceptance. No, he would *never* accept what she'd pulled.

Especially when he was drunk, he'd plot and scheme ways to seek his revenge. For example, he knew a guy who knew a guy who knew a guy who'd whack her without a second thought. Or he could hire a private eye to do the kind of surveillance that would pull up something he could use to blackmail *her*. Better yet, he could leak whatever they dug up to the press and ruin the bitch for good. A soberer head prevailed, though. The bottom line was that Susie Sheppard just wasn't worth that much effort, let alone any jail time, and frankly, he was glad not to have to deal with her on a day-to-day basis.

Besides, the best possible revenge was to ensure that *Dana Point* flourished without her; that the ratings not only stayed steady but soared; and that, eventually, the fans would forget about her and shift their loyalty to someone more deserving. To that end, Burt had only one goal: find an actress who embodied the soul of the show, and the fans' hearts and minds would follow. However, they'd been auditioning all week, and so far, the auditions had not yielded an actress with the presence, looks, and acting chops to accomplish all that.

Until now.

The casting director had introduced her as Tally

Jones. She had large, luminous brown eyes, high cheekbones, graceful elegance, and a shyness that bespoke an endearing vulnerability. Her cute little nautical getup drove home the fact that she'd fit right in on the *Dana Point* set. In fact, she looked so perfect for the role of Jamie that Burt was almost afraid of what would come out when she opened her mouth.

He needn't have been. Her reactions to the stiff, sullen read by the casting director were spot on, and Burt was enthralled by the subtle nuances of even her smallest reactions. When the line demanded anger, she didn't growl it with the heavy theatrics of the other actresses who had auditioned for the role or as Susie would have done if the line had been hers.

By the end of her last line, she had him in tears, and not just because she was so damn believable but because he knew that Susie would be *so damn pissed* when she realized how easily he'd replaced her.

After Tally finished her reading, the room was silent for a moment. Then, in unison, all eyes turned to him.

Burt smiled. "That's our Jamie. My dear, welcome to the Burt Tillman family."

As the rest of the execs gathered around *Dana Point*'s newest addition to congratulate her, Burt took his leave.

It was three o'clock: happy hour.

Chapter 9

STEVE SMILED AND nodded and murmured all the right phrases to let Tally know that, yes, he was proud of her and that this stint on *Dana Point* was only the beginning of a lot of good things yet to come. Then Tally dropped the bombshell: the role wasn't for just one episode or, for that matter, a multiepisode arc. Nope, Burt Tillman wanted to sign her to a five-year contract.

Steve kept the smile on his face, even as his heart nosedived into his gut. *It's the beginning of the end. She's on her way up, which means she's on her way out, too.* Then came the salt in the wound. The contract wasn't even being sent his way but to Josh Gold's office. Because *he* had sent her up for it.

She was very apologetic about everything, but she was not above pointing out that the audition had somehow missed his radar. "I know I owe you a lot, Steve. And of course, I still want you to manage me. But the way I see it, an actor needs to take any and every opportunity that comes her way, no matter where it comes from."

"Well, of course." He nodded vigorously. "With Josh in the picture, I can start taking care of the details. You'll be shocked at how many there are."

Clearly relieved that he understood, Tally stood up to leave. Impulsively, she leaned over Steve's desk and gave him a kiss on the cheek.

Yep, it was the beginning of the end.

"Way to go, babe." Josh parked himself on the corner of Sadie's desk. "So, when do I meet my new client? Tally—what was her last name again? Johnson?"

Sadie laughed. "*Jones.* Gosh, I hope you don't forget it when you meet her. She should be here within the hour. She can't wait to sign that contract."

"I don't blame her. Hey, is she your new roommate? You know, the one with the big tits?"

Sadie's face turned deep red. "No, smartass. That's Mandy. But you can rep her, too, if you'd like. She'd be honored."

"Ha! Yeah, I'll bet! With headlights like hers, she should troll for roles on the other side of the hill, in the Valley. If she gets big enough there, we can mainstream her. You know, make her the next Jenna Jameson."

"Jeez, Josh! Don't say that about Mandy. She's a classically trained actress."

"Oh, really? Does she call the right one Rosencrantz and the left one Guildenstern? Because that's as close as she's ever going to get to Shakespeare, unless someone's producing *Juliet Does Dallas.*"

Sadie swatted him off her desk. "You're so disgusting! Look, I still have to make those last few changes to Tally's contract, so why don't you get back to work, so I can, too?"

"You know you love it when I talk dirty. Just admit it." Josh gave her a lopsided grin. "Seriously, though, don't you think we should celebrate our new account? Go ahead and make us reservations at Dan Tana's. Say, nineish."

Sadie nodded nonchalantly and waited until he'd gone into his office before picking up the phone. She didn't want it to be too obvious to Josh that she was thrilled he'd asked her out.

Or had he? *Is this an official date, or is it just Josh's way of fighting off his loneliness?* she wondered. *Does it really matter?* When she really considered the question, she knew the answer was no. She was falling in love with him, and to her, that was *all* that mattered.

By the time Mandy made it to the *Dana Point* audition, the role had already been cast.

"Sorry," the receptionist murmured. She seemed mesmerized by Mandy's chest. Nothing new there. Mandy was getting used to the stares. "We called your agent. We presumed he would have passed along the message."

Mandy nodded. She couldn't tell the woman that her cell-phone service had been cut off the day before. That was OK with her, though—she was tired of getting calls from the credit-card collection agencies, anyway.

She prayed she'd make it back to the parking meter before she got a ticket. When she'd parked, she hadn't had time to rummage through her purse for any quarters before the audition. She stuck her hand in her purse now to see if indeed she had a few quarters left to her name. No coins appeared; instead, she came up with Jerry Conover's business card.

She stared down at it for what felt like a long time. She'd never thought of herself as a prude; she certainly enjoyed sex, and lately she'd loved the lust she saw in the eyes of men who passed her walking down the street. *Who says porn has to be raunchy, anyway?* she thought. *Great acting could bring it to a whole different level.*

She looked down at her car's gas meter. Only a quarter of a tank left, just barely enough to get her to Chatsworth.

She had to pay her bills somehow. If it meant being an extra in a porn flick or two, well, so be it. Who watched those things, anyway?

Traffic was hellish all the way out to the Valley. When she finally arrived at her destination, she discovered that Dandy Candy Productions was located in a nondescript low-rise office building. *This isn't so bad,* Mandy thought. *And the parking is free, so that's a plus.*

The offices were elegant inside. And busy. The receptionist, a pert girl in short-shorts and a cropped T-shirt that rode up to the base of her high, perky breasts, seemed tethered to her headset. She motioned for Mandy to fill out a form on a clipboard. *Just what I need, an audition in which I'll be dissed by some porn director.*

She was still filling out her audition information sheet when Jerry strolled through the reception area. Seeing her, he stopped short. "Great! You made it."

"Yeah. Um, look, Jerry, do I have to audition?"

He smiled. "We're all cool here. Why don't I show you the setup?"

Relieved, she put down the clipboard and followed him down a hall lined with double doors. Over each set of doors was a light fixture; a couple of the lights glowed red. He pointed up to them and said, "We're filming in those studios."

"How many studios do you have?"

"Eight total. Four here and four in the west wing."

"Wow, you have two whole wings?"

"Porn is big business, Mandy. But we're different from the other companies in that we like to do it tastefully."

Tastefully. She liked the sound of that.

"We can take a peek through one of the viewing rooms if you'd like." He motioned for her to follow him through a side door.

What she saw made her blush: a naked man, down on his knees in front of a woman in an ass-grazing sheer red negligee. Behind them was a heart-shaped bed with a tall headboard. In front of them, three cameras, all at different heights, were following the action from every possible angle. It was obvious that the man—the actor?—was going down on his scene partner.

Jerry tapped her lightly on the shoulder. "Would you like a drink?" He held out a glass of wine.

Figuring that if she was going to actually do this, she'd certainly need some liquid courage, Mandy said, "Sure, thanks."

As she gulped her wine, she grew more fascinated with the actor's technique. At least, she thought it was his skill that was making the actress moan with such pleasure. As he burrowed deep inside her, one of his hands meandered up toward her mountainous breasts, which had somehow made it out of the thin, low-cut shell of her negligee. The actor stroked one of her nipples until it stood up.

Mandy's breasts responded, too, just watching the scene. *Wow, I guess these films really* are *a turn-on.*

Mandy didn't remember Jerry refilling her glass, but she was grateful that he had.

"Why don't you get undressed? You'll have to eventually." He grinned knowingly at her.

She paused for a second, then slowly unbuttoned her blouse and stepped out of her skirt. Jerry scrutinized her as she stood there in her bra, panties, and heels.

"Nice. You've got a rockin' bod. Believe me, I'd know," he murmured. "Whattaya say I introduce you to your cast mates?"

She blushed. "But—but I don't know my lines! And what's my motivation?"

He walked over to her and stood close—*really*

close. "Do you mind?" He didn't wait for her to nod before he unclasped her bra, which fell to the floor. She wondered whether or not she should pick it up but decided not to. It was a good decision, because just then, Jerry leaned into her, and odds were they would have bumped heads.

Gently, he cupped her breast in his hand. She responded with a shiver. He stroked it for a bit, then let his hand roam to the flat part of her stomach. He didn't stop until he reached her panties.

"I'd say you're motivated, wouldn't you?"

She laughed. "Um . . . yeah. I guess you're right."

"If you need a plot, the one they're shooting is simple enough. He's the boy next door, who came over to borrow a cup of sugar. He's getting more than he bargained for. Then again, so is she. Otherwise, it's all improv. Think you can wing it?"

"Sure, that sounds simple enough."

He took her hand and pulled her into the studio with him. When he yelled, "Cut!" the cameramen stopped rolling.

He walked Mandy over to the bed. "Frankie, Celia, this is Mandy. Frankie, I want to see how she does in your capable hands. Celia, you can take a break for now. Oh, and toss Mandy your nightie, will you?"

Celia nodded. She lifted the negligee over her head and held it out to Mandy, but she had to clear her throat to get Mandy's attention. Mandy was too busy staring at the one thing she couldn't see when Frankie had his back to her: his penis. It was the largest she'd ever seen.

She slipped on the negligee as Frankie smiled proudly. He knew he'd impressed her. Then, very gently, he pulled her down onto the bed with him.

She did nothing as he stroked her face. In due time, his hands wandered over her breasts, and he sucked on one until the nipple poked straight out of her nightie. Satisfied with the results, his hand trailed further down her body, until it was between her legs, and then inside her. She arched up and moaned.

He took that as permission to slip off her panties and plunge deeper and deeper. Then, without missing a beat, his fingers were replaced by his cock.

She squealed when it entered her. At first it hurt, but soon it felt so *goooood*. When she climaxed, she wasn't acting. The second and third orgasms were real, too.

Eventually, somewhere in her dulled consciousness, she heard Jerry yell, "Cut!" The cast and crew were suddenly animated—laughing, talking, and, best yet, complimenting her for her authenticity. And for her tits.

One of the cameramen turned to Jerry and said,

"They looked great on camera. I got in close when he was sucking one. You should see her face, too."

It suddenly hit Mandy that she hadn't uttered one line of dialogue except for all the dirty talk that came out of her mouth when Freddie entered her. Talk about improv!

"You'll be sore tomorrow," Jerry warned. "We shoot again on Friday. Freddie plays a fireman, and he saves the damsel in distress. What do you say, are you in?"

Mandy nodded.

And to think I get paid for this!

Chapter 10

EVERY MORNING BY seven, *Dana Point*'s hair and makeup trailer was a beehive of activity. In the two months since she'd gotten the role as Jamie, Tally had learned to show up there early. Not because she wanted to be first in line to get prettied up but because she loved watching the hustle and bustle that went along with making the show.

The set was a village in miniature. Besides the show runner, Chase Bracken, there were nine other writers who shaped the twenty-four-episode season, and each episode was helmed by one of the show's five directors. *Dana Point*'s cast included eight stars and eight costars and myriad support players and guest stars. Any given episode could have as many as thirty actors on the set, plus an army of a hundred or more crew members.

In the skilled hands of Conrad, who headed up the three-person makeup department, and Garfield, who oversaw two other hairstylists, a certain magic took place in the hair and makeup trailer. All it took was the right pancake base, wig, or lipstick shade to transform the actors—all just ordinary people like herself—into characters known and loved by millions of fans.

It was also the prime venue for the kind of drama that comes with having fifteen or so neurotic, high-strung, and (for the most part) egocentric lead actors, all of whom want their fair share of the hourlong dramatic series' limited airtime: just forty-four minutes for each episode, to be exact. With such a large ensemble cast, obviously not every lead actor was in every scene. In fact, if the story line didn't revolve around them, a few of the actors might have just one or two scenes in any given episode, if any.

Apparently, Tally was one of the luckier ones. She was being positioned as a lead as opposed to a secondary character, which gave her as many as eight pages of dialogue to memorize on each of the eight days it took to shoot a single episode of *Dana Point*. She relished every moment of it.

Airtime wasn't the only perk she was enjoying; Tally had to pinch herself the first time she walked into the trailer assigned to her on the Royalton lot. She couldn't believe that she didn't have to share it with anyone. She was also afraid to leave anything in it at first. What if the producers came to their senses and realized they'd made a mistake? Soon, though, it felt like her second home. In fact, she liked it much more than her tiny Studio City apartment, and she promised herself she'd look for a nicer place as soon as she paid off her credit cards. Maybe she'd even replace her beat-up old Honda; the fee that Josh had negotiated for her was more than she'd ever thought she'd make in a year, let alone for a single episode.

Even though she was slowly settling into her new life, she still feared it would all just disappear one day. She'd read of that happening to other young actors. They presumed their shows and careers would last forever and spent every penny they made on clothes, jewelry, fast cars, and cliffhanging Hollywood Hills homes with eye-popping views of Los Angeles and the ocean beyond. Usually, they partied hard as well. This got them into the tabloids, which helped their careers. Then, for whatever reason, their series were canceled or their movie careers flatlined, and they had to sell everything just to survive. Tally was determined not to let that happen to her. She always came to the set ready to play out her lines from a variety of emotional angles, and between scenes, she'd retreat to her trailer, where she'd check and recheck her lines.

Needless to say, her scenes came at the expense of some of her cast mates'. When lines and scenes were cut—as they often were—tempers flared and snapped.

"Watch yourself, missy," Ben Kendrick, the makeup artist assigned to Tally, whispered in her ear one morning as he applied a set of lashes. "Valerie is on the warpath. The costume department wanted to put you in something red, and she just threw a fit! Apparently, the color was too close to the dress she's wearing today." Ben gave a naughty giggle. "As if anyone will be looking at her two-thousand-dollar muu-muu when you're onscreen!"

Tally tried hard not to wince lest her lashes end up crooked. "That's cruel, Ben! I think she looks just fine. She's not much bigger than a size six."

"Doll, have you lost a contact or something? OK, fine. Maybe you're right—after she's put on her third pair of Spanx. Seriously, I'm amazed that she has never passed out on the set." He arched an eyebrow.

Tally casually glanced across the makeup trailer to one of the hair stations where Valerie Rendell, who played *Dana Point*'s revered society matron, was seated. "Why would she care, anyway? I've only got one line in that scene, and we stand in the same frame for less than a minute."

"That's not the point. On a set like this—on *any* set, really—egos clash over the silliest things. I tell you what, the catfights I've seen would curl your hair without hot rollers." He sighed. "When that drama mama Susie Sheppard was here, someone ended up in tears *every single day*. And it was never Susie, I promise you that." He leaned in, to be absolutely certain that only she could hear him. "That girl knew how to get her way around here. God, she was a handful—in more ways than one, if you catch my drift."

Tally didn't exactly know what Ben meant by that, so she just nodded.

He took a large powder brush and swept it over her cheeks. "Then again, it's all of the drama that makes our work so intoxicating, isn't it? You can just *feel* the passion in here, can't you?"

"What passion?" Tally looked around at the others. Sure, a couple of her cast mates were chatting together, but most were reading their lines or yawning after late-night antics that had already made that morning's gossip columns.

"You've got to be kidding me!" Ben leaned in closer. "There are at least three cast affairs going on right now. But you didn't hear it from *me*. You know what they say: if you see the trailer rockin', don't come a-knockin'."

Shocked, she tried to guess who he was talking

about, but she couldn't even imagine. Half her cast mates were married, and most of the others were seen in public on the arms of just-as-renowned significant others.

Just then, Conrad walked by and tapped his watch, then jerked his thumb toward Justin, the actor who played Tally's old high-school boyfriend on the show. Ben, somewhat miffed, gave him a dismissive wave. Justin certainly didn't seem to be in any hurry. He was too engrossed with his BlackBerry to care about when he'd get his turn in the makeup chair. Tally guessed he was posting a Tweet; many of her cast mates were obsessed with their fan counts on Twitter or Facebook. In fact, Sadie had told Tally to get Steve on the ball with opening and managing her own accounts, but these days, she found it hard to get Steve to do anything other than escort her to the many events where she was now on invitation lists. Meanwhile, she was getting tired of being polite and asking him to come along. It would be nice to go with someone else for a change.

But who? she wondered. If Ben was right, even a "friendly" cast mate might not be receptive to hanging out with her. *I need a real life,* she thought, then remembered she barely had time to take care of herself, let alone meet someone new.

Ben leaned in close to touch up her eye shadow.

"Have you taken a peek at Perez's blog today? He claims he's got insider info that your fan mail has been spiking. If that's the case, Valerie won't be the only one pissing and moaning about you."

Tally was confused. "But everyone has been so nice to me."

"That won't last forever, love." Ben frowned. "All I'm saying is that you'd better watch your back. A sweet thing like you can get stepped on easily in this town."

Ben was right. A half-hour later, when she walked onto the set, she noticed a frost in the air. She was sure it had to do with an Awful Truth "Blind Vice" item, posted just that morning, hinting that Tally had been dissing Justin to one of her gal pals in the ladies' room of the Tower Bar the night before. Justin confirmed her suspicions, and his form of passive-aggressive retaliation was to mug at her while she taped her close-ups.

After she blew her line for the fifth time, Carl Norman, the episode's director, called, "Cut!" and gave her an exasperated look. He walked over to her and whispered, "Jeez, Tally, get with the program. It's one simple line, for God's sake."

"I know! I'm so sorry."

For a split second, she wondered if she should tell him about Justin's prank. But she knew Justin would only deny it, and worse, the crew would dislike her for being a tattletale. So she kept her mouth shut.

All I want to do is show up on time and do my job, she thought. *That shouldn't be so hard, should it?*

One thing that did make the job a bit easier for Tally to put up with was the thrill of seeing some of her favorite actors who also worked on the Royalton lot. Including Gabriel McNamara.

Even seeing him on the billboard plugging his show, *Intensive Care,* on the wall near the studio gates made her blush at the thought of their kiss at the *Vanity Fair* Oscar party.

And during the few times, like now, when she saw him in the Royalton cantina, she shyly turned her head in order to avoid eye contact. She would never presume that he remembered her from that night. Even so, a little voice inside her wondered why *not* say something to him? What would be the harm in that?

But she was simply too timid, and she had to admit that she would prefer it if he did remember her. What a thrill it would be to have him walk over and say, "Wow, so I was right! You made it, Tally."

Should that happen, she imagined she'd smile adorably and say something witty and flirtatious.

"Hey, look, I hope you don't mind—"

Shaken from her daydream, Tally looked up from her script to see Gabriel standing there right next to her.

She was so startled that she forgot she was holding a cup of iced coffee. Otherwise, she would not have jumped straight up in order to shake his hand, and maybe she wouldn't have spilled it all over the hospital scrubs that were his usual attire for the show.

Gabriel cursed and jumped back as a big, dark wet spot formed on his scrubs.

"Oh my God! I'm so sorry. It's just that—well, you startled me."

"The costume department isn't going to be happy about this," Gabriel replied, but his lopsided grin showed he wasn't too worried about it. "I just came over to ask you if—"

"Yes, yes! Of course I remember you!" She could feel herself turn pink for jumping the gun like that, but she couldn't help herself.

"OK. Well." He seemed taken aback. "Does that mean you'd like an autograph?" He patted the pocket of his scrubs top. "I don't seem to have a pen on me—"

Omigod, she thought. *He thinks I'm some rabid fan!*

"No! I mean . . . we've met before." She waited for some reaction from him, but his eyes were still void of any recognition. She frowned. "Isn't that why you came over here?"

"Not exactly. We were hoping to borrow this." He pointed to the empty chair beside her.

For the first time, she noticed that he wasn't alone. Allison O'Connor, the tall, beautiful, auburn-haired actress who played his love interest on *Intensive Care,* was trying hard to conceal her smirk.

Tally shook her head regretfully. "Oh! Of course. Take it. In fact, I—I have to get back, so if you need this table, to—" She fumbled for her purse but only succeeded in knocking it off the table and onto the floor, sending the contents flying under their feet. "Oh, no!" She scrambled to grab her makeup and keys, but she refused to chase the loose change that had rolled under the other tables around them.

As soon as she'd gathered all of her things together, she made a beeline for the exit. Gabriel called after her, but she headed out the door anyway. She presumed a pen had rolled out of her pocketbook and he wanted to return it—with his autograph.

It wasn't until she got back to the set that she realized she'd left her script in the cantina. Not wanting to go back to the scene of her humiliation, she was just about to see if she could cajole one of the production assistants into retrieving it when she heard a knock on her trailer door. Assuming it was someone calling her to the set, she opened it. But it wasn't a PA.

It was Gabriel.

She stepped back as he came through the door. "You found me! How did you . . ."

He laughed. "Your name is on your script." He handed it to her. "You're the girl from the *Vanity Fair* party, am I right?"

She nodded. "So, you do remember."

"Well, to be honest with you, I remembered your name." He pointed to where it was typed neatly on the cover of her script. "It's somewhat unique."

"Yep. I guess it is."

He smiled as he leaned up against the door. "You made quite an impression that night."

"Apparently, it wasn't that great," she answered flippantly. "Look, thanks for returning the script. They'll be calling me any second now—"

He didn't believe her. If he had, he wouldn't have taken her into his arms and kissed her again. It was just as she'd remembered the first time: both gentle and passionate. All thoughts went out of her head, except that she never wanted him to let her go.

As if reading her mind, he jerked her even closer to him. She felt them falling together onto the large-cushioned couch that was the focal point of the trailer, and in no time at all, her blouse was over her head. She should have been worried about where it had fallen when he tossed it aside and whether it was getting wrinkled, but she wasn't. Nor did she wonder if he was smearing her makeup. She seemed to have lost all perception of time and place as his lips trailed down her neck and over her breasts.

She did gasp, though, when she felt his teeth on a nipple. "Please! We can't—"

"Am I your first?"

"*What?*" She couldn't believe her ears. "Are you asking me if I'm a virgin? Of course not!"

He smirked. "So, you've made it in your trailer before?" He seemed intrigued by the thought.

"No, of course not!" She shoved him away. "I don't think it's appropriate."

"Too bad." He sounded disappointed, but he still held her firmly.

"I think you should let me go." Even as she said it, she could hear the uncertainty in her voice.

Obviously, he did, too, because instead, he pushed his tongue past her lips and into her mouth. At the same time, his thumb circled her breast, and his other hand inched up her thigh, beneath her skirt.

She didn't wear Spanx. She didn't need them, and this made it much easier when his hand pulled down her panties and wandered between her legs.

Seeing the open lust in his sky-blue eyes, a million thoughts went through her head, all at once: how much she loved seeing him on the screen; her shock when she'd discovered he'd been watching her scrounge under the bushes during the *Vanity Fair* Oscars party; and how she had burned with desire for him when he'd kissed her that night. Her final thought, however, washed over her like a cold sweat: *Is what Ben said true? Do these trailers really rock back and forth when someone is making love?*

Because of the production assistant's loud rap on her trailer door announcing that she was wanted on the set, Tally wasn't about to find out.

She jumped straight up off the couch. In a way, she was relieved. Yes, she wanted to make love to Gabriel McNamara, but she didn't want to be a between-scenes trailer quickie.

Gabriel groaned but took the hint. After he gave her a long, slow kiss to remind her of what she'd just missed, he said casually, "I'm sure we'll see each other around."

And that was it. He was gone.

It was Tally's turn to groan. Too bad she didn't have time for a cold shower.

In her next scene, she was supposed to kiss Justin. Instead, she devoured him. Afterward, he stuttered out an apology for having ruined her close-ups that morning and admitted it was totally unprofessional of him. Besides, he said, what actor was stupid enough to believe the tabloids, anyway?

Tally was. At least, she allowed herself to believe a certain blind item that ran a week later in the *New York Post*'s Page Six column that asked: "Which hunky TV heartthrob wants to play doctor with the newest leading lady in nighttime dramas? It shouldn't be long before he drives home his (Dana) point."

So why hasn't he called? Tally wondered.

Chapter 11

WHERE IS SHE?" Josh Gold was almost afraid to ask, but he had to know. That was his job: to rein in his insane clients and to read them the riot act when necessary. And Susie Sheppard was the nuttiest one of them all.

"Susie's killin' me, dude." Calvin Walsh looked awful. He was bone-thin, ashen, and disheveled. If Josh hadn't known better, he'd have thought the man was starring in a remake of *Night of the Living Dead* instead of directing *M*A*S*H*U*P*.

That Susie had somehow gone off the deep end was the last thing Josh wanted to hear. He thought this was going to be a simple case of holding Susie's hand and giving her a pep talk, and quite frankly, he was too tired for anything more than that. The flight from Los Angeles to Cairo was a grueling seventeen hours, with a two-hour stopover at London's Heathrow Airport. He'd considered taking some coke with him, even if it meant stashing it in some not-so-pleasant body cavity, but Sadie had convinced him that the last thing he wanted was one of the airport's security dogs sniffing his overnight bag, let alone his butt.

"Look at it this way," she'd said. "The trip is a full day to get there, a day to talk sense into Susie, and a full day of flying home again. So you go cold turkey for three days—nothing wrong with that. If you're lucky, you'll break the habit. It's not good for you, anyway."

As always, she was right. But at the moment, he could have killed for a couple of lines.

He stared down at the director. "What the hell is going on here, Calvin? I get this frantic call from Paramount telling me that I'd better get my ass over to Egypt, pronto, to see what's up with you guys! They made it sound as if one of the pyramids had imploded."

"If that bitch client of yours had her way, one just might." He shivered. "What she did to that poor camel . . . Well, let me just tell you right here and now, I never want to see that woman again. *Ever.*"

Josh frowned. "What are you talking about? What camel?"

"Don't ask, Josh. You *don't* want to know." Calvin

ran his hands through his hair—or what was left of it. "Look, she and I haven't talked since the camel incident, and as far as I'm concerned, if I never speak to her again, it will be too soon." He looked Josh squarely in the eye. "Even before that, she was complaining about everything: the script, the heat, her wardrobe, even the *sand!* And she bitched out the lead practically every day, claimed his breath stank, and then she had the audacity to come on to him on the one day his wife was visiting the set. And that was just because she wanted to upset *her lover.*"

"Wait a minute." Josh couldn't believe his ears. "I thought you and she had a little thing going on."

"We did—at first. Until she came on to the cinematographer. No, wait. Before him, it was that Israeli security dude. Or was it the Lebanese caterer? Aw, hell, I don't remember. *The woman is insatiable!* She's also a troublemaker. She lies to everybody about everyone else, and the rest of the cast hates her guts. Did you know I've lost *two* tranny Klingers because of her? Both guys said she was too emasculating! As if I didn't know that already. And because of her shenanigans, I'm nearly three weeks behind schedule. My crew is ready to walk! Not to mention that the camel master refuses to bring another one of his animals on to the set until she's out of here. He says he'll come back after the 'devil lady' goes. That's what the natives here call her, by the way. Quite a term of endearment, isn't it?" Calvin shook his head in horror. "Look, Josh, the bottom line is, *I need the camel.* It's irreplaceable, whereas Susie Sheppard isn't. And anyway, Scarlett has already agreed to step in as Hot Lips. She just wrapped her last scene on *The Avengers,* and we're working around her until she can get here."

Josh couldn't believe his ears. His client was being replaced! If the press got wind of this, she'd have a hell of a time getting any work at all in Hollywood, let alone transitioning from TV to film. "So, how did Susie take the news when you told her?"

"Why do you think you're here, you moron? That's why you get paid the big bucks." Calvin opened the tent flap and pointed down toward the end of the row of tents. "Last one on the right."

Susie did not take the news well.

She cursed and screamed so loudly that many of the exotic birds in the area stayed away from the oasis that surrounded the set for almost a week afterward. At least, that's what was reported on Page Six.

On the flight back, Susie spent so much time in the plane's lavatory that Josh wondered if she'd smuggled on any of the cocaine he so desperately needed in some orifice. He considered asking her, but then he remembered Calvin's curious references to camels, and he thought better of it.

Besides, he got his answer when he saw her emerging from the lavatory with the dude who had been sitting across the aisle from them. The guy was some Texas oil executive traveling back home from Riyadh, and as he walked out, he zipped up his pants with a shit-eating grin.

That did it. Josh was pissed. When she reached their seats, he hissed, "You're ruining your reputation! You don't think that creep is going to boast to his drinking buddies that he made it with Susie Sheppard?"

She gave him a pout. "Big deal. What if he does? Who'll believe him, anyway? Men like that never get lucky with women like me."

"That's the point. There *is* no other woman like you! Look, Susie, I'm warning you to cool it. When word gets out about your antics, you can forget about having a film career. No director in his right mind will want to hire you."

"To hell with movies—for now, anyway. My therapist told me I was rushing things a bit, putting my television career on ice so quickly."

"Your shrink said that?" Josh didn't even know she was seeing one. Well, that was somewhat of a relief. There might be hope for her yet. "So why didn't you listen to her?"

"It's a him. And I didn't listen because I don't respect men who have Oedipal complexes."

"How would you know he has an Oedipal complex?"

"Because he screams out his mother's name when we have sex, silly."

Well, there went any hope Josh had that he could count on her shrink reeling her in.

"And it's all your fault, Josh, nudging me to take a role in that vile movie! It's going to flop, you know. Calvin Walsh is a *freak*. He can't get a hard-on to save his life." She opened her purse and pulled out a compact. "In fact, I think I should go back to *Dana Point*."

Josh stared at her in disbelief. "Get real. Do you actually think Burt Tillman will welcome you back with open arms? What were you smoking in Cairo?"

She gave him a knowing smile. "The stuff was sublime. If you want, I'll turn you on to my source there."

He paused for a moment—but *just* a moment. "I'll pass. Besides, Burt has written off your character and introduced a new one."

"Yeah, yeah, I know. I also know that *you* represent this new girl . . . what's her name? Tilly? Trudy? Oh, right, *Tally*." She dabbed at her nose with a puff. "As if I were so easily replaceable! What a naughty boy Burt is, to even think that."

"The ratings don't lie, Susie. And so far, it looks like Tally is a winner."

Susie stopped admiring herself in the compact's mirror to glare at Josh. "We'll see about that. Don't you worry, Burt will do whatever I tell him. And what I'm going to tell him is that it's time for Katherine to make a miraculous recovery from that coma."

Whatever she's got on Burt must be a real bombshell, Josh thought. "If you pull that off, then more power to you. It'll be a miracle, but you'll be the biggest diva on the small screen."

"That's the game plan." She smiled smugly. "And while I'm reconnecting with my fans, you can secure me another film deal." She pulled down her eye shade. "Something where I can really shine. Only next time, no animals. Been there, done that."

Josh let that one slide. There were just some things he really didn't want to know about his clients, and he had a feeling this was one of them.

Chapter 12

WHEN THE PUBLICIST Steve Fisher hired for Tally asked her if she wanted to be one of the celebrity drivers in Long Beach's annual charity event, Racing for the Kids, she had said yes immediately. The sponsor, Toyota, had committed to giving a very large donation to the charity of her choice—the children's hospital in her hometown of Corvallis, Oregon—if she would agree to participate, and to Tally, giving back to the community was one of the most important obligations that went along with fame.

All of the celebrity drivers were supposed to show up promptly at eight o'clock the Saturday morning of the race. Mandy and Sadie had both agreed to go with her and to act as her pit crew. When Mandy showed up on Tally's doorstep in a breast-hugging wifebeater and short-shorts, Sadie raised an eyebrow and said, "You know, Tally might actually win this thing. When all the other drivers get a look at you in that getup, they'll drive straight off the road."

Mandy smiled as if she'd just been paid a huge compliment. "Hey, do you think they'll let me wave the checkered flag?"

Tally laughed. "I'll put in a good word for you."

"Just be sure to introduce me by my porn name. If they've heard of Taylor Made, I'll be a shoo-in."

"I don't know about that, Mandy. I mean, this is a family event." Tally checked her watch. "Omigod, it's already past seven! We'd better hit the road. Even on a Saturday morning, the 405 can be a bear."

Sadie yawned as she climbed into Tally's backseat. Josh had kept her up late last night, but for all the right reasons. No client business, no angsting over his Machiavellian partners, just the two of them in his big, fluffy bed overlooking Malibu Beach. "The way you drive naturally, you'll get us there with time to spare," she said as Tally sped toward Long Beach. "You Oregon farm girls drive *fast*."

Tally smiled. "Yep, there are some advantages of growing up in the sticks, including fast cars and a lot of empty back roads to race them on. When my parents heard I'd be racing, they were thrilled. My dad figures since the county sheriff couldn't catch up with me, outracing a few celebrities should be a piece of cake. Buckle up, ladies."

On the drive down, Mandy regaled the girls with the nuts and bolts of how a porn film gets shot. "Apparently, I'm good at it. Already, two of my movies are on the top ten list of popular porn rentals, according to *Adult Video News*. The producers have offered me a contract!"

"Wow!" Sadie exclaimed. "So, let me ask you a question that's always bugged me about porn. How do those guys stay . . . well, you know, *ready* all that time?"

Mandy laughed. "Sometimes guys need a fluffer to keep themselves hard. But apparently, that hasn't been the case when I'm on the set." She puffed up proudly.

Tally gave her a quizzical look. "What's a fluffer?"

Mandy giggled. "It's a person who keeps the male actors all hot and horny between takes. Usually, it's a woman who plays with herself or someone else— or with him—until I get back on the set. But if the actor is gay, then it's another man who's the fluffer." She looked down lovingly at her breasts. "Most of my costars are straight, so Mary Kate and Ashley seem to do the trick every time."

Tally sighed. "What is it with men and boobs? It's got to be some kind of primal chemical thing."

Sadie perked up. "Speaking of chemicals, I think Josh has finally broken his cocaine habit."

Tally gave her friend a thumbs-up in the rearview mirror. "Sadie, that's great! How did that happen?"

"His trip to Egypt was a great start in weaning him off the stuff. Also, I made sure his coke dealer's calls never got through to him. But the biggest factor was when I put my foot down and told him I was walking out if he didn't quit."

"He certainly cares about you, Sadie," Mandy said reassuringly.

"Yes, I know he does. In fact—" She paused and took a deep breath. "Well, I was going to wait until after the race to tell you, but I can't hold it in any longer. Josh has asked me to marry him!"

Upon hearing the news, Tally swerved off the road for a second, causing the trucker behind her to honk his horn. She waved her apology in the rearview mirror. "Oh my God! Sadie, I'm so happy for you!"

Mandy squealed. "When's the wedding? Can we be bridesmaids? Does this mean you'll quit your job?"

Sadie laughed. "Well, we're thinking later in the summer. And yes, both of you are my maids of honor. As for my job, as soon as I find my replacement—and let me tell you, it'll either be a guy or a *very* homely woman—I'll have time to plan our wedding." She smiled sublimely. "And the rest of our lives together."

The rest of their lives together. Tally let that sink in. *Mandy and I are just starting our careers, and Sadie is in a committed relationship. I'm so glad we're all so happy . . .*

So, why, all of a sudden, did she feel so alone?

When they got to the racetrack, Tally was given a hot-pink helmet with a matching one-piece racing suit to wear on the track. The *Dana Point* logo was embroidered on her breast pocket, and her getup fit as snugly as a catsuit. This netted her admiring glances from the other celebrity drivers, including Gabriel McNamara.

"You look so hot," he murmured into her ear as all the celebs—the two of them, along with Patrick Dempsey and Eric Dane of *Grey's Anatomy*, Chelsea Handler, and thirteen others—posed for a group photo.

In response, she smiled pretty and slapped his helmet shield so that it fell down over his face.

It had been three weeks since their encounter in her trailer, and he hadn't bothered to stop by again, let alone call her. Granted, she hadn't had time to give him her number, but still, he could have gotten it just by having his publicist check with her publicist if he'd wanted it badly enough. Which, obviously, he didn't.

Good, Tally thought. *Then he won't be too upset when I beat him.*

The route circled around downtown Long Beach. The drivers were supposed to go ten laps. *A piece of cake,* Tally thought.

She let Gabriel take the lead for the first four laps. By the sixth, though, she was right on his heels, and by the seventh, she was half a lap ahead and planned to stay that way. Just to tease him, she'd allow him to get close, but then she'd peel away. She also played chicken with him, just like her high-school boyfriend had taught her. Because his helmet's shield was down, she couldn't tell if she was impressing him or making him angry. *What difference does it make? I've got nothing to lose if I beat him. In fact, I'll have a lot to gain—my pride, for one thing.*

On the last lap, he turned up the heat. While the other drivers played it safe, Tally and Gabriel were neck-and-neck to the finish—until he spun out. A sickening feeling washed over her as she watched his car turn several 360s before coming to a stop on top of a median.

Shocked and feeling guilty, Tally pulled over to the curb, then jumped out and ran over to his car. By the time she'd pushed her way through the crowd, the emergency safety crew was already attending to him. When he saw her, though, he beckoned her over. She put her hands on his face; it was her way of saying *I'm so, so sorry*. Taking one of her hands, he brought it down to his lips and kissed it. Even with all the cameras clicking around them, all she could think of was the fact that she would have been heartbroken if anything had happened to him.

Jason Bateman might have won the race, but it was Gabriel's lips on Tally's hand that made the cover of the Calendar section of the *LA Times* the next day.

Chapter 13

TALLY FELT SHE owed it to Gabriel to make sure he made it home safely to his place in Malibu. Saying so out loud to Sadie and Mandy earned her their snickers, but Tally stuck to her guns. "You never know! He bumped his head pretty hard."

"Hey, we get it. You want to be sure he doesn't pass out on the road on the way home," Sadie said as she elbowed Mandy. "Not that his publicist could do that, right?"

Tally shrugged, tossed Sadie the keys to her car, and never looked back.

Gabriel allowed her to drive without protest. Cautiously, she took the 405 North to 10 West and then crawled along with the rest of the weekend traffic going north on the Pacific Coast Highway. Although he insisted that she could go faster, she thought they had both had enough racing for one day.

Finally, they arrived at his house, a postmodern cottage squeezed into the center of Malibu Colony Drive, with only a sand dune or two separating it from passersby on the beach, of which there were plenty.

When she walked inside, she was shocked. The house was so cluttered! She wondered why he hadn't hired a maid, then figured he just hadn't had the time. *I can certainly understand that,* she thought. She noted that a narrow trail had been cleared through the boxes and magazines that filled the living room and followed the path further inside.

When she saw the wall of plastic bear honey containers, she stopped dead in her tracks.

Gabriel, who was kicking through some of the debris, turned around to find her staring at it in awe. Before she could even ask the question, he said, "It's a little hobby of mine, collecting those. Just something I do for fun with my niece. It started out as a joke. You know, 'Let's see how many of these we can collect.'"

"OK." Tally didn't know what else to say. She decided that in a way, it was touching that he'd do something cute like that. For his niece.

She also noticed that none of the windows had

shades, blinds, or curtains and commented that it must get pretty bright. "I like it like that," Gabriel explained. "I love lots of sunshine."

Tally wondered if the photographers loved that, too—especially when Gabriel insisted that they make love at the window looking out onto the ocean.

"Look at that sunset," he said as he kissed her neck and shoulders. "It's like we're all alone here, at the end of the earth."

She nodded as she allowed him to strip her of her racing suit.

How funny, she thought. *Of all the souvenirs I've collected, this jumpsuit will mean the most to me, because it was what I was wearing the day we made love.*

She stood there in her bra and thong but not for long. Very slowly, he pulled down one bra strap, then the other. Then, kneeling before her, he hooked a finger into her panties and slowly pulled them down her legs.

The thong teased her skin as he inched it toward her ankles. When he got to her feet, he lifted one up and pulled the sliver of silk off its heel, then kissed it. He then did the same with the other foot.

She wanted him *so badly* now, and when he looked up, she saw the desire in his eyes, too.

She was less genteel, tearing at the zipper of his

racing suit and shoving it off his hips, along with his boxer briefs, before throwing herself into his waiting arms.

Their kiss seemed to go on forever. When their lips finally parted, he scooped her up and took her to the only piece of furniture free of any clutter: a low-back armchair that faced the big picture window. Placing her behind it, he moved her hands onto the arms of the chair. Bent over the top of it, she could see him admiring her ass in their reflection in the window.

Gently, he nudged her feet away from the chair before entering her from behind. His thrusts started out slow but soon were faster as he dug deeper inside her. She moved in unison with him, arching her bottom even higher, taking more of him into her, closer to orgasm with each stroke. Just as they came, together, the sun dipped below the horizon.

Happy, sated, and exhausted, Tally fell back into his arms. He seemed surprised, but he held her there for a moment. Then, instead of leading her upstairs to his bedroom, he cleared a place for her on the couch.

She must have dozed off, because when she opened her eyes, it was already dark outside. Surprised that she was alone, she called out his name.

No answer.

Then she saw a note on the coffee table. *Had another engagement. Please leave through the back door, it's the only one not on a spring lock. Have a nice night.—G.*

Furious, she wondered how he expected her to get home. Sure, she could call a taxi, but she didn't even know the address to give the dispatcher. Why hadn't he just woken her up and offered her a ride home?

Tally angrily grabbed her clothes off the floor and threw them on. She stuck her head out the front door to look at his house number, but there wasn't any. She'd have to go out to the mailbox to figure out where she was. It was out by the curb, so she propped the door open with her shoe. Two steps later, she learned the door was too heavy for the shoe as it shut behind her, trapping her shoe—and her purse—inside.

Damn it! There was nothing she could do but start hobbling up the street. Maybe she'd recognize someone driving by, and they'd let her use their phone. Or maybe they'd recognize her first, then tell everyone that she was a one-heeled ditz.

A ditz who'd just gotten used by Gabriel Mc-Namara.

She was halfway up Malibu Colony Drive when she remembered that Josh also lived in the Colony, just a little bit down the road. Well, at least her agent would take her in, and Sadie would be there, too. They wouldn't laugh at the fact that she'd just been used . . . but the look of pity in their eyes would hurt just the same.

The next day, Gabriel sent her purse to the set, accompanied by flowers. The note on the card read, *Miss you. Hope you feel the same way.*—G.

Of course she did, but she didn't want to admit it to herself.

A week later, when he finally called, there was an urgency in his voice. "I've got to see you, Tally. I've been thinking about you all week."

She knew why, and it made her uncomfortable: he saw her as a booty call. She should have been angry, but instead she was, well, *flattered*. Because it meant he still desired her.

Sadie was aghast. "Look at you! You're acting like a naive schoolgirl! Have you forgotten that he totally ditched you after sex?"

"He might have already had plans. Was he supposed to just break them because of me?"

Sadie nodded emphatically. "He would have, if he *cared*."

"He's Gabriel McNamara, for God's sake! I'm still thrilled he even knows I exist."

"And you're Tally Jones—or have you forgotten that? Sure, he's a big, established television star. But guess what, Tally: You're on TV now, too. So start acting like it!"

Tally knew she was right. But she wasn't going to chance losing Gabriel by playing hard to get. He was handsome, successful, and, according to the latest issue of *People,* the "Sexiest Man Alive."

So she agreed to see him, determined to bide her time and give their relationship room to develop.

"There's a guy across the street holding a camera with a telephoto lens," Tally murmured out of the corner of her mouth to Gabriel. They were sitting at a curbside table at the Urth Caffé on Melrose. In the month they'd been seeing each other, the place had become one of their usual hangouts. Unfortunately, because it was a favorite haunt of a lot of stars, a caravan of paparazzi was always waiting there.

Tally hated the fact that since she'd started going out with Gabriel, her every step outside the walls of Royalton Studios was dogged by people with cameras. In fact, last week, she'd found out that her landlady had been tricked into letting some guy into her apartment who claimed he was supposed to put in a new Internet cable connection. Nothing was missing, but later a narrated video appeared on YouTube in which someone walked around her apartment and commented on her bedroom ("Is this where she and Gabriel McNamara go at it?"), her closet ("Wow! She kept her cheerleading outfit from high school! How sick is that? I wonder if she wears it for Gabriel"), and the contents of her fridge ("Yogurt and diet Coke? *That's it*? Someone, please, buy this poor girl a meal!").

She felt violated. She knew she had to find another place, somewhere more secure. In truth, she was hoping that Gabriel would ask her to move in with him. But he never did.

They were sleeping together, and the sex was hot, torrid, and rough—but never loving. The rest of their relationship was empty as well. Whenever they were in public, Gabriel acted as if he couldn't keep his hands off her, and needless to say, the press picked up on their "love affair" in no time flat. But he could go from hot to cold in an instant, and she constantly felt as if she was walking on eggshells. Their tumultuous on again/off again relationship was tabloid catnip, and whatever it lacked in actual affection was made up for in column space.

It helped that they were spotted at all the usual celebrity hot spots: clubbing at Avalon and the Tower Bar, hiking in Runyan Canyon, shopping at the Grove or on the Robertson Boulevard or grabbing a quick bite at Urth. Tally would have much preferred the kind of notoriety that comes with a respected career, not sensationalized press. Why not go somewhere more private, where they might actually be able to pass as civilians, or at least somewhere they'd be left alone? She would not have minded at all if they'd gotten their coffee and food to go, and on more than one occasion, she'd even suggested that they stay in at Gabriel's place and she'd make breakfast there, but he seemed to prefer to go out.

It suddenly dawned on her that he might actually like the attention of having his picture taken, and OK, fine, it was part of the lives they led. Still, that didn't mean she had to like it.

"Where is the camera creep?" Gabriel asked. He started to rise from his chair, but Tally reached across the table and held his hand so that he wouldn't go after the guy, which he had a habit of doing.

"Leave him alone, please, Gabriel. Let's just pretend he isn't there."

"OK, sure. I'll do this instead." He leaned into her and gave her a deep, long kiss. They could hear the shutter of the camera snapping away. As soon as Gabriel pulled back, the pap walked away. "See? Problem solved. He got what he came for." Gabriel went back to sipping his latte and reading the *LA Times* sports pages. The kiss had been all for show.

Tally frowned. "Just because he got what he wanted doesn't mean you had to stop."

He looked up from his paper. "Getting a little needy, are we?"

She glanced away before he saw the tears in her eyes. "Forget I said anything."

"I won't forget. You know I love it when you get all riled up. Makeup sex turns me on. Why don't we go back to my place?"

No way. She wasn't going to settle for friends-with-benefits sex, with no love attached. Today she wanted them to be a normal, happy couple, doing normal, happy things. Putting on a cheery smile, Tally said, "Hey, I have a great idea. Why don't we go to a movie? The new James Cameron flick just opened at the Arc-light."

"Sure, OK. We can grab a seat in the back, like last time."

Tally shook her head. "I don't want to see our picture in *Us* with your hand down my shirt again."

His lips curled into a naughty smile. "Can I help it if I can't keep my hands off your breasts?"

"Well, you don't enjoy them enough to sleep with them." She looked him straight in the eye as she spoke. It was a big issue between them that he didn't invite her to sleep over and that when she insisted that it was too late to leave, he asked her to sleep in the guest room.

Gabriel didn't flinch at her jibe. In fact, he smirked.

"It's a waste having them beside me when my eyes aren't open to admire them." He folded his paper and stood up. "On second thought, I think I'll go home and watch the game."

"What, you don't want to spend the afternoon together?"

"Sure I do, if you want to watch the game with me. Or have sex."

Tally frowned. This wasn't going at all as she'd planned. "Look, I'm sorry for what I said about the movie. I don't mind if we sit in the back row—"

"Chill out. I wasn't going to take you, anyway." With that, he sauntered off toward the car.

Now she wished another pap had been around ready to take their picture, because if Gabriel had seen him, he would have leaned in to kiss her, and she could have dumped her cappuccino on his head.

She could play to the cameras, too.

Chapter 14

BY THE TIME Susie had gotten back from Egypt, the tale of her *M*A*S*H*U*P* fiasco had reached epic proportions. The whole town was buzzing about how she'd been a diva, how she'd almost caused Calvin to have a nervous breakdown, how the cast had despised her, how she used the international crew as her personal harem, and then there was *the camel incident*.

In Hollywood, where myth trumps reality, this alone was enough to get any producer to think twice about hiring an actress for a commercial, a walk-on, even a reality show. *The Amazing Race* was a nonstarter, for crying out loud. Josh felt it was a last resort, but he was still shocked when the producers told him in no uncertain terms that his client would never be welcomed aboard. As one of the show's producers put it, "Susie Sheppard? You've got to be kidding me! She's a one-woman wrecking crew. We have to get our cast and crew in and out of fifteen countries in any given season. We can't afford an international incident."

That might have upset Josh, but Susie wasn't fazed at all. "Now are you ready to talk to Burt about putting me back on *Dana Point?*" she asked as she paced the floor of his office.

The clacking sound of the six-inch stilettos of her Christian Louboutin leopard booties on the parquet wood floor was giving Josh a headache, but he wasn't going to give her the satisfaction of knowing that. Instead, he shrugged and said, "Sure, whatever." What did he have to lose, anyway? Worst-case scenario, he could drop her with no regrets, knowing he'd done everything he possibly could for her. And if she was right, he'd take the credit for having revived her career. It was a win-win situation.

"Before you go, I have a little present for my old pal Burt that I'd like you to give him for me." She pulled out a black cardboard box wrapped with a big, beautiful bow. "Tell him it's my way of making amends—and for saying thanks in advance." She smiled innocently at Josh. "Oh, and by the way, I hear congratulations are in order. You're getting married?"

Still convinced that Burt was a long shot, Josh was

relieved to change the topic. "Yep, to Sadie, my assistant. I couldn't live without her. I guess this proves it. You remember her, right?"

"Of course." Susie was lying. Other people's assistants were as insignificant to her as insects—unless she could coerce some important tidbit out of them about their bosses that she could use against them at a later date.

Josh kept going on about his betrothed. He told Susie how Sadie had once tried her hand at acting "before she came to her senses." He laughed. "In fact, if you pull this off, you'll be on set with one of her closest pals, Tally Jones—"

All of a sudden, Susie was all ears.

"Oh, really, they're close buds?" Susie said sweetly. "How cool is that? Now I can't *wait* to meet her! In fact, I insist on throwing Sadie a little bridal shower. Just us girls, you know? You're getting married when? Next month, right before the Emmys? Perfect! I can throw something together really quickly. In fact, we'll do it next weekend. Tell her I'll be calling her to get the guest list. And don't look so jealous, big boy. I tell you what: your bachelor party is on me, too."

That's certainly generous of Susie, Josh thought. *Maybe Egypt was a wake-up call for her, after all.*

Was it his imagination, or did her teeth resemble fangs?

Before she left his office, Susie said, "Oh, and Josh, let's keep my plans to return to *Dana Point* quiet. I think it's important that we keep our mouths shut until the actual day I start work. Please don't even mention it to Sadie."

Josh thought she seemed to be putting the cart before the horse, but he agreed. As he made his way toward Royalton Studios, he wondered what might be inside the box. It was too light to be a horse's head, but he had no doubt that it would have the same effect on Burt. It had crossed his mind to open the box and see what was inside, but he thought better of it. No need to be an accomplice to another one of Susie's crimes.

Like everyone else in Hollywood, Burt Tillman had heard that Susie was back in town, with her tail dragging between her legs. Or *something's* tail. Burt shuddered at the thought.

Burt sat patiently as Josh made his pitch. In fact, many of his points were valid, such as how easy it would be to bring Susie back into the fold, since the Katherine character was only in a coma, and how the publicity would boost the ratings right in time for May sweeps. Not to mention that, since both Jamie and Katherine were supposedly in love with Hank, it might make for a series of compelling conflicts between the two characters (a.k.a. great catfight material).

And most important, Josh concluded, Susie so badly wanted to make peace between the two of them.

Burt smiled at Josh. "Sorry, buddy. I'm not buying it. You know better than anyone how great Tally's been for the show. Why would we need Susie back? You can use any excuse you want with her, but the truth of the matter is this: that bitch will never work on another Burt Tillman project again."

Well, that's that, Josh thought. He had done his best, but it just wasn't going to happen. Unless Susie was right, and the black box in his hand held the key to her survival in Hollywood.

"I hear what you're saying, Burt, believe me. Still, I'm honoring Susie's request. She wanted me to give you this, as a token of her appreciation for all your past efforts on her behalf and any future consideration." He placed the box on Burt's desk.

Burt looked as if Josh had handed him a bomb. He didn't open it. Instead, he jerked his head toward the door. Josh had worn out his welcome.

As the door closed behind him, Josh hoped Burt wouldn't hold whatever was in the box against him or any of his other clients. Then again, if what Susie had on him was that great, maybe he'd use it against Burt himself one day.

When the time came, he'd ask Susie to disclose her dirt.

It took half a bottle of Crown Royal before Burt had the nerve to open the box. When he lifted the lid, there they were, the pictures taken on that awful, awful night, along with a note: *Forgot to mention that I e-mailed these pictures to myself. Ooops, my bad! Hey, what do you say to tripling my per-episode fee and putting me in every episode? You do the math. Your primetime princess is back!—Susie.*

He had no choice.

Josh wasn't even off the Royalton lot before Burt reached him on his cell: "I've got to talk it through with the writers, but let's say she starts a week from Monday. Just give her this warning: *No shenanigans.*"

Yep, the bitch is back, and on even better financial terms than before, Burt thought. By the time he finished his bottle, he was sobbing like a baby.

Sadie wasn't exactly thrilled that Josh had taken Susie up on her offer to throw a bridal shower, and she said as much to Tally and Mandy, who were sunbathing with her out on the deck of Josh's house. "I don't even know the woman. Why would she do this for me, anyway?"

Mandy, who had been checking out the man candy walking by on the beach, poked Tally to get her attention at one of the finer specimens within eyesight before answering. "Look, with all the bad press she's been getting lately, my guess is that she's figured out she needs all the friends she can get right now."

Tally nodded as she slapped Mandy's hand away. As far as she was concerned, she was off the market. She wondered if Gabriel felt the same way. "Frankly, I think it's a very sweet gesture. Besides, Sadie, she's one of Josh's clients. If you say no, it will put him in a difficult position."

Sadie sighed. "Well, the good news is that she wants to plan it all on her own. All she's asked is that I supply the guest list. Since she's one of my aunt Essie's favorite actresses—don't ask me why—I'm sure she'll be thrilled that Susie's doing this for me." She smiled brightly. "And considering all the other details I've got to manage, why look a gift horse in the mouth?"

The invitations arrived the next day, printed on thick cream-colored stock and embossed in gold. The shower was to take place a week from Saturday, in one of the bungalow suites at the Beverly Hills Hotel.

How posh, thought Tally.

For the event, she chose a chiffon dress by Jean Paul Gaultier. It was short and sleeveless, with thin straps and tiered tulle ruffles along one side. By the time she arrived, most of the guests were already there and milling around the bungalow's living room, laughing and talking. It was a small group, twelve at the most. Sitting in the various chairs and on the two facing couches were Susie, Mandy, and Sadie, as well as some actresses Tally immediately recognized, all of whom were Josh's clients and currently starring in various television shows or feature films. Granted, Sadie knew them all, but she wasn't really close to any of them.

Even more strange was the fact that none of Sadie's family was there. When Tally greeted her, she noticed there were tears in Sadie's eyes.

"Where are your mom and your sister?" Tally asked. "Where's your aunt Essie?"

Sadie tried to shrug it off. "Apparently, none of my family was invited."

"An oversight," Susie purred in Tally's ear.

Tally turned around to face the hostess, and what she saw was pretty intimidating. Make that frightening. Up close, Susie's face was stretched so thin it seemed to have the texture of fine lined porcelain. The older actress was known for her beautiful features, but from where Tally was standing, the symmetry of her face was unnatural. When she held out her hand, Tally pretended she didn't see the pronounced veins.

"Ah, so glad you made it! Josh sings your praises endlessly. I have been really looking forward to meeting you. But no time to talk now, the entertainment is about to start."

"Oh, great," Tally said. "I love all the silly parlor games people play at bridal showers. You know, the don't-say-a-word game and the one with the balloon—"

"Oh, I've got something a lot more fun for us than a few silly balloons. But *shhhhh!* It's a surprise." She gave Tally another once-over. "Frankly, dear, I'm saving the best surprise for last. And it's just for *you.*"

Tally forced a smile onto her face and resisted the urge to shiver.

Just at that moment, the lights dimmed, and a Lady Gaga song came on over the in-room speakers. Everyone went silent, and the anticipation in the women's eyes said it all: *A male stripper? This might be fun.*

But instead, two women entered the living room from the bedroom, wearing nothing but wedding veils, G-strings, and six-inch white stripper shoes. Their silicone-stiffened breasts, which protruded from their bodies unnaturally like heat-seeking missiles, made them look like live Barbie dolls. Or maybe it was their hair, which was like straw in both its color and its texture.

The guests didn't know whether or not to laugh. Most glanced over at Sadie for a clue, but the shocked look on her face proved she was just as mortified as they were. "Is this some kind of sick joke?" she asked no one in particular.

It got even worse when the strippers pulled out canisters of whipped cream and proceeded to smother each other in a gooey lather before taking turns licking it off. While some of the guests snickered or rolled their eyes in disgust, a few remained frozen in shock.

Only Mandy seemed enthralled by the performance. Sadie nudged Tally. "I think Mandy is actually taking notes on their technique."

Tally felt Susie's eyes on her. When she glanced over, Susie gave her a knowing wink.

Why is she staring at me so intently? Tally wondered. She shivered again as she remembered Susie's promise to give her a very special prize.

When one of the strippers made the mistake of squirting whipped cream on her breast and offering it up to Sadie, the bride-to-be gave her a look that sent her scurrying off to the other side of the room. But she was soon back, this time holding something behind her. "My, my, my, what do we have here?" she asked in a cheery voice. "Sadie, does this remind you of anyone?"

She then revealed a very large two-headed dildo. Each girl took one of its heads in her mouth and proceeded to give it quite a moan-and-groan workover.

"The natural blonde is pathetic, but the other one's got some technique, for sure," Mandy whispered to Tally.

"Just don't offer to give her lessons," Tally hissed back. "Sadie will kill you. Frankly, after today, I wouldn't be surprised to find Susie's body bobbing out in Los Angeles Bay."

Mandy shrugged, and after the women were done with their show, she handed the more skilled of the two her business card. "Give me a call. I'll set you up with my agent," she murmured.

Just when Tally thought it couldn't get worse, Susie did the unthinkable. She grabbed one of the girls and dry-humped her, straddling the woman between her legs as if she were a prized bronco. Then she pulled the other stripper onto her lap and cupped her breasts for good measure.

Was this an act? No, it couldn't be. Susie looked as if she was enjoying it too much.

Tally and Sadie hug onto each other in horror. They couldn't believe what they were seeing.

Sadie whispered, "I guess Josh wasn't lying when

he said Susie would screw anyone at any time. I just thought he meant, you know, to get to the top!"

"Well, look at the upside," Tally said. "Aren't you happy now that your aunt Essie's invitation got lost in the mail?"

Noting Sadie's disgusted look, Susie slithered over to her. "Something wrong, sweetie? Oh, let me guess. This sort of thing just doesn't do it for you." She clicked her tongue in mock regret. "Oh, well, win some, lose some." She let her hand glide down Sadie's arm longingly. "But fair is fair, right? I just didn't want to short-change you, so I gave you the exact same party I threw for Josh last night."

Sadie turned to stone. Josh hadn't come home last night, and now she knew why.

Tally, Sadie, and Mandy looked at one another as they all had the same thought at exactly that moment: *Was Susie at that party, too?*

The girls couldn't get out of there fast enough. Just as they reached the door, Susie sidled up to Tally. "Now for the best surprise of all: we'll be cast mates! I'm returning to *Dana Point*."

"Oh. That's . . . nice." Tally smiled, but her gut took a dive. She couldn't believe her ears. She remembered what Ben had said about Susie: *When she was on the set, someone ended up in tears every single day.*

She was beginning to understand why.

Chapter 15

DEPENDING ON WHICH of the entertainment rags one read, Susie's return to *Dana Point* was either a triumph or a tragedy. *People* heralded it as "The Comeback of the Decade," while *The Hollywood Reporter* declared, "Been There, Done That: Is *Dana Point* on Its Last Legs?" One thing was certain: everyone was going to watch it. Susie's comeback was a television event not to be missed.

And didn't she just know it.

She had one goal in mind as she basked in the attention: get Tally off the show. But it wouldn't be easy. The cast and crew had tremendous respect for the younger actress, so getting rid of her would take a major case of sabotage.

That meant starting at the top. Even before she showed up on the set, Susie called Burt Tillman with some specific demands. "Darling Burt, we have to milk my return for all it's worth, don't you think? After all, everyone will be looking at *me*. Why take the focus off the star? This little actress you hired as Hank's temporary love interest . . . what's her name again . . . oh, yes, *Tally*. I presume you want to start moving her out now, am I right? Please tell wardrobe no D&G, Marc Jacobs, Gucci, Gaultier, Cavalli, Versace, or Herrera for her. Why waste designer clothes on a secondary character? Off the rack is good enough, don't you think?"

Burt had no intention of phasing out Tally, but he didn't have the guts to say that to Susie. Instead, he said, "Sure, Susie, whatever. I'll talk to Gladys in wardrobe."

Thanks to what Susie had on him, all he could do was sit back and watch the carnage.

Dana Point's show runner, Chase Bracken, was next on Susie's list, and she arranged to meet him for dinner at the Polo Lounge the night before her first day on the set.

Susie's last stint on the show had taught Chase to be wary, but when he got to the restaurant, he was surprised—make that shocked—to find a sweet, meek Susie ready to greet him in a back banquette. She was up on all the story lines and complimented him on how exciting she thought the show had gotten that season.

"Boy, I so miss being a part of a show with such great writing!" she said. She touched his hand gently when she talked and hung on his every word as he filled her in on what was coming up.

"Wow, it sounds like we'll be ending the season with a bang! And now that Katherine is to be resurrected, I guess you can alter that episode this way—" As Susie made her suggestion, her hand, which had been idle between them on the banquette bench, inched its way up his thigh. Chase shot straight up at attention, but he didn't scoot away.

Nor did he come up with an excuse for why he had to get home to the missus and their caterwauling twin toddlers when Susie asked him to walk her to her car or when she suggested that he follow her back to her place. By the time he got home the next morning, she had his mind spinning with ways in which her role could be massaged and enlarged.

Susie's first day on the set was tense. The hair and makeup trailer was as quiet as a morgue, as all of her cast mates—including Tally—waited for her to appear. When she arrived, she came bearing gifts: wonderful little bazaar trinkets from what she called "my little vacation away from all of you, my friends here on *Dana Point*."

Everyone knew what she really thought about them. Still, it was always better to stay on Susie's good side, so they all smiled and were effusive in their thanks. "So sweet of you to think of me." "We've missed you, honey." "The place wasn't the same without you."

Air kisses all around. Long live the queen—but keep clear of her guillotine.

Soon it was obvious to everyone that Susie was after Tally's head. The rumors about Tally started almost immediately. Because Susie was the set's prima diva, the head of makeup, Conrad, personally did her face, while the key hairstylist, Garfield, handled her coiffure needs. When Susie was in their chairs, they snickered and stared at Tally, then passed along Susie's venom to anyone who was within earshot.

One rumor making the rounds had Tally asking the production assistants to act as go-betweens with her and her dope dealer. Another had her spreading gossip that one of the show's directors, Larry Hornsby, had come on to her in her trailer, and she had to fight him off. When Larry heard this, he refused to work on a script in which Tally was involved. Whether it was true or not, he was on his third marriage, and two alimony payments were enough for him.

Insecure Justin, one of Susie's on-set favorites, practically cold-shouldered Tally whenever she was near and shrugged off any attempts she made at small talk. Tally later found out that someone had told the press that she thought he had body odor.

Valerie, who already had it in for Tally, practically took up residency in Susie's trailer between breaks, and the icy stares she shot at Tally from her perch in the hair and makeup trailer made the younger actress tear up.

Needless to say, the tabloids eagerly picked up the gauntlet. The headline on the cover of *In Touch* asked, "Is Tally Jones *Dana Point*'s Good Girl Gone Bad?" and the accompanying article included the supposed evidence—all a fabrication on Susie's part, of course.

Tally was wounded and bewildered.

As Ben lined her lips, he set her straight. "My God, doll, you don't need to be a shrink to figure out what's going on. You're following in her footsteps! She views you as a threat." He lowered his voice to a whisper. "And considering her personal history, I guess it's no wonder."

Tally was all ears. "What? Don't hold back."

"Well . . . let's just say she's got some Mommy issues. Her mother was the original arm charm, one of the most beautiful women in the world. She had the world-class lovers to prove it, too: Euro-trash royalty,

not to mention a few actors you might have heard of."
He cupped Tally's ear and whispered names that set
her head spinning.

"Next to her mama, poor Susie looked like a pug,
but Mommy dearest made her into the Barbie doll you
see before you. She had any flaws nipped and tucked
into oblivion: a new chin here, a new nose there, a
real forehead—and don't forget breasts, even though
Mother Nature did. When she came to town, Susie
was almost androgynous. Let me put it this way: she
was a tomboy in more ways than one." He gave her
a wink. "Then Mommy gave her daughter's virginity
to an Arab prince as a gift. That should be enough to
screw anyone up for life."

"Oh my God!" Tally sat straight up in the chair.
"That's just *terrible*!"

"Well, as you can imagine, it was enough to send
little Susie off the deep end. Ever since, she has been
determined to one-up her *mamacita*."

Tally couldn't believe her ears. "How do you know
all this, anyway?"

"Listen up, Sleeping Beauty, this is old news—and
from the highest authority there is: *Vanity Fair*. That
issue sold more copies than the one after Princess Di
divorced Prince Charles."

Tally glanced out of the corner of her eye at Susie.
"Now you're making me feel sorry for her."

"Don't. Seriously, Tally, thanks to who she is and where she comes from, she believes all threats have to be annihilated. Right now, that means *you*. And you should never forget that."

Tally frowned. "If that's the case, then how can I fight back?"

Ben held up a hand mirror for Tally. "Darling, it's simple. *Just keep being you.* Sweet, talented, and lovable. Susie is none of those things, and you've got it all."

He took both her hands and pulled her out of the chair. "Now, go do your thing!"

Ben was right. All she had to do was be herself. She was pleasant to everyone, from the little old lady at the craft services table all the way up to Chase Bracken himself—despite the fact that he'd cut down the number of her scenes and the way he treated her as if she were an interloper on the set.

Tally didn't complain about her off-the-rack costumes, either, although it did really piss her off. After all, it was just her character's wardrobe. Instead, she overhauled her personal wardrobe by familiarizing herself with Los Angeles's trendiest underground boutiques, where she purchased pieces that were both elegant and cutting-edge from rising designers. Now she didn't mind when the photographers shouted out her name for a quick snap or two, and she even developed her own pap strut, so that even when they went for a "candid shot," she always looked happy and put together. Invariably, *InStyle* included her on their "What's Right Now" list, and she always scored five stars in E! Online's Fashion Police column. And when Steve called her with the news that she'd been offered a Maybelline cosmetics contract thanks to her "great look," she was ecstatic.

Most important, Tally approached every minute of airtime as if it would be her last. She came prepared, and she played to the camera.

All of her efforts counteracted Susie's sabotage. The viewers loved the younger, more accomplished actress. In fact, Tally got three times more e-mails from fans than anyone else on the show—including Susie—and that was all Burt needed to be able to inform Susie that, sorry, the studio suits insisted that Tally be under contract for a long, long time.

Susie's response was to slam down the phone.

Burt didn't care. Instead, he demoted Chase (of course, he knew that Susie had somehow gotten to the show runner) and ordered the new show runner, Jack Putnam, to put the two actresses in as many scenes together as possible, so that the audience could watch the sparks fly.

Chapter 16

ON THE DAY the Emmy nominations were announced, Tally got a call at five in the morning.

"Have you heard yet?" Sadie squealed.

Tally, still half-asleep, mumbled in response, "Heard what?"

"You've been nominated for Outstanding Supporting Actress in a Drama!"

Tally bolted straight up. "Oh my goodness!"

"Do you know what that means? You're golden! That bitch Susie can't touch you now. Not that she ever really could. Hey, listen, Josh wants to talk to you . . ."

Whatever Josh was saying to Tally took too much

concentration for her to process. She listened to him ramble on and on about what she should expect over the next two months until the award ceremonies, but by the time she hung up, all she could think about was how proud she was.

And how proud Gabriel would be when he heard.

On the set, the news that Tally had been nominated for an Emmy put her in a whole different realm. She became *Dana Point*'s new golden girl.

"I can't believe it," Tally told Ben. "Steve and Josh are getting calls from all kinds of people—film directors who want to work with me, companies who want to give me stuff or have me represent their products. And all of a sudden, everyone is being so nice to me again!"

As he stood back to admire his handiwork, Ben beamed down on her like a hen looking at its favorite chick. "Get used to it, princess. When you make it big in Hollywood, life opens up like the petals of a big, beautiful flower. It's as if you're one of the popular kids in school or you've won the lottery. 'No' suddenly becomes 'Yes, ma'am.' You'll be invited to every party, every talk show, and to present at every awards ceremony. You'll walk the red carpet at every premiere. Designers will give you free clothes, and restaurants will save you the best tables. All because only three things matter in this town: fame, power, and money. But remember, *money trumps all.*"

Money. Right now, she felt as if she had all the money in the world. Steve had recently hooked her—and many of his other clients—up with some hotshot financial manager named Tanner Bascom, who was investing her money in all sorts of things she didn't understand: derivatives, futures, commodities, stocks and bonds . . .

When she told Mandy about Tanner's investment strategy, her friend sniffed. "Sounds like a bunch of hooey, if you ask me. Just do what I'm doing. Get into real estate. Land is solid. It'll always be there. Worst-case scenario, you can live on it. Try doing that with grain futures!"

Mandy had a point. In the six months since she'd been working in the "adult entertainment" industry, as she called it, she'd already bought a house in the Hollywood Hills enclave of Outpost Estates and invested in several older apartment buildings in the Valley. Tally, on the other hand, hadn't even gotten out of her Studio City apartment.

"Admit it, Tally. You're waiting for Gabriel to ask you to move in with him," Mandy said, slightly disapprovingly. "Well, he's never going to do that, so you might as well look after yourself."

Tally knew her friend was right. Still, she wanted to hear it from Gabriel.

Strangely, in the three days since the Emmy nominations were announced, she hadn't heard from him at all. Suddenly, it hit her: unlike the year before, he had not been nominated in his category, Lead Actor in a Drama. *He's got to be disappointed,* she thought. *Maybe I should go see him, to make sure he's all right.*

That night, she drove to Gabriel's after work. There was a light on in the house when she pulled up. She rang the doorbell; it took him a while to answer, and when he opened the door, he was naked except for a towel wrapped around his waist.

"Oh, I'm sorry! Were you taking a shower?" she asked, slightly embarrassed.

"I was about to jump into the hot tub," he said, giving her a lazy smile. "Care to join me?"

Relief surged through her body. He didn't seem to be jealous about her Emmy nod after all. She was glad. Still, she knew *one* of them had to bring it up, and if he wasn't going to do so, it would have to be her. "You heard the news, right?"

His eyes narrowed as the light in them went out. He shrugged. "Oh, yeah, your nomination. Congrats." He knotted the towel even tighter around his waist. "So, about the hot tub. Are you in or out?"

There was a chill in the air, but it wasn't from the

salty mist rolling in from the ocean. She hesitated just a second before going into the house.

So, he is jealous. "Look, Gabriel, I know you're happy for me, and I appreciate it. I feel very lucky that I even got nominated. What an honor—"

"You're not practicing your speech on me, are you?"

That hurt her feelings. "No, of course not. I was trying to make you feel better, is all."

"Thanks, but I don't need your pity." He moved in close to her. With a finger under her chin, he lifted her face to his and leaned in for a kiss.

A second later, a female voice called, "Gabriel, are you coming into the tub or what? Oh! You have company." Tally opened her eyes. The other woman's damp hair clung to her scalp and her shoulders. Like Gabriel, she was wearing only a towel, but just barely.

Upon seeing her, Tally pulled away from Gabriel. "I guess I'm interrupting something. I'm sorry." She didn't even recognize her own voice because it was quivering so badly.

"Wow, you're Tally Jones! I just love you in *Dana Point*!" The woman looked over at Gabriel. "I thought you said the two of you had broken up?"

Tally's shock turned into rage and quickly began to boil over. If they had broken up, she hadn't been told! The last thing she wanted was to hear it from a stranger. A stranger who was apparently sleeping with her boyfriend.

She's lucky I don't toss her out of here on her ass, Tally thought.

But Tally didn't live there. She wasn't even welcome to sleep there. *What am I doing here, anyway?*

She walked out the door without looking back.

"Tally, honey, don't you get it? He's jealous of you." Sadie sucked in her gut so that Mandy could zip up the dress. It was about the fortieth wedding gown she'd tried on that afternoon. She stuck out her tongue at her reflection in the floor-length mirror, then motioned for Mandy to unzip her again. "Think about it. You get a nomination, and he doesn't. He doesn't even bother to call you to congratulate you. All of a sudden, you're the new hot talent. Do you know what that does to his ego?"

Mandy tugged hard at the zipper until it finally made its way down Sadie's back. "Let's be real," she said, eyeing Tally in the mirror. "He's been treating you badly since even before the Emmy nod. Is he even worth it?"

Tally shook her head. "I get that he's upset, but I thought he'd be happy for me. What he did is just such a disappointment."

Mandy shrugged. "Do what I do when I'm upset. Buy yourself something. Preferably something expensive."

"I already have." Tally gave her a sly smile. "Sadie, how many more dresses do you have back in the dressing room?"

"Thank God, this was the last one. I give up! The wedding is only three weeks away, and I still haven't found a dress I like. I guess I'm getting married in my pajamas." Sadie sighed. "Oh, well, at least everything else is under control. Why do you ask?"

"I want to take you two for a little ride."

Sadie tugged her jeans on under the dress, then slipped out of the white taffeta concoction. "Let's blow this joint."

The girls piled into Tally's car, and she started driving. Tally refused to answer questions as she worked their way up winding roads, eventually stopping at a rambling ranch perched on a canyon ridge high over Beverly Hills, on Mulholland Drive. It had stucco walls, a terra-cotta tile roof, and lush vegetation all around. Best of all, it had a pool out back from which you could admire the view all the way to the ocean.

After showing her friends around the property, Tally raised her hands in triumph. "Three bedrooms, three baths, a humongous kitchen, a gate to keep out nosy photographers—and it's all mine! What do you think?"

Sadie was speechless, but Mandy exclaimed, "Tally, it's perfect! I am so jealous."

Tally laughed. "If it makes you feel any better, Steve thinks I paid too much for it. In fact, he's worried I might have overextended myself."

Sadie guffawed. "He's got nothing to worry about. Between the Emmy nomination and how Josh renegotiated your contract for more money, you can easily cover the note on this place. When do you move in?"

"This weekend." Tally walked to the edge of the pool. As she dipped her toe in the water, a ripple flowed out and moved, in concentric circles, toward the center of the pool. Watching it reminded her of her life: growing beyond any bounds she ever thought had constrained her.

"It's time, don't you think? And not a moment too soon."

Chapter 17

WHILE ALL OF Hollywood was prepping for the Emmys, Sadie managed to pull together a beautiful wedding. The invitations, engraved with silver script and made by Tiffany & Co., invited guests to the Malibu cliffside estate of a music producer who was lending it to Josh and Sadie for the day as his wedding gift. The cake was a chocolate sponge filled with chocolate truffle cream, and its white icing was flavored with Grand Marnier; pale silver roses cascaded down its three tiers.

"Your dress is beautiful, Sadie, and it fits you perfectly," Mandy murmured in awe. She was right. It was an A-line Vera Wang, and soft flounces swirled below the silver off-center bow at the waist. It had an asymmetrically draped portrait neck, and whereas one of the satin straps seemed to be held in place by an off-kilter bow, the other fell off her shoulder onto her upper arm, giving the dress an element of effortless glamour. Completing the look, she carried white roses tied with a satin silver bow that complemented the Badgley Mischka silver sheaths overlaid in sheer chiffon with sheer cap sleeves that Tally and Mandy wore.

Sadie's only regret was that the wedding could not have been more intimate. She would have preferred just family and friends. Instead, industry obligations meant Josh's clients and partners, not to mention some other noted actors, producers, studio heads, and directors, were all included on the guest list.

Still, Tally had never seen her friend so happy.

Just as the sun crested the horizon, Tally and Mandy preceded Sadie down a white carpet strewn with silver-tipped rose petals. Sadie's train-length veil fluttered in the gentle breeze as she made her way toward Josh, who waited for her under a flower-bedecked huppah. The setting sun's golden glow reminded Tally of the first time she'd made love with Gabriel. She knew he'd been invited, and she quickly scanned the rows of guests sitting in chairs on either side of the aisle.

Steve Fisher was there; he gave her a curt nod,

then wrapped his arm around his latest protégée, a young woman who slightly resembled Tally: brown hair, broad shoulders, and a sunny smile. Her nose, though, was a little off-center, and Tally fleetingly wondered how long it would be before Steve persuaded her to go to one of the many plastic surgeons listed in his little black book.

Randall Littlefield was there, too, although Sadie hadn't taken lessons from him in months. Tally gave him a slight nod. She'd yet to take Randall up on his offer of private lessons. Now that she was on a show, she just hadn't had the time. Maybe before the new season . . .

Tally knew she could count on Susie Sheppard to come in something inappropriate, and Susie did not disappoint. She sported a white dress, a white fox fur coat, and big Christian Dior sunglasses. *Besides the bride, no one wears white to a wedding,* thought Tally. For Susie's sake, Tally hoped she was on her best behavior. Otherwise, Mandy might follow through on her threat to toss the actress into the champagne fountain. "Control the urge," Tally warned her. "In Susie's book, no press is bad press, so don't indulge her."

Gabriel was nowhere to be found.

She shouldn't have cared. In fact, she should have been relieved that he hadn't shown up. Instead, she felt sad, and somewhat lonely, especially when Josh lifted Sadie's veil and recited, "With this ring, you are made holy to me, for I love you as my soul. You are now my wife."

Tally knew this should have been one of the happiest times of her life. Her career was catching fire, her dear friend was getting married, and she had just moved into her dream home.

But she had no one with whom to share it, which made the void seem even bigger.

The band, which was called Andree Belle, was a jazz-salsa combo with a sultry female lead singer. Sadie and Josh had heard them one night at Nic's Martini Lounge in Beverly Hills and had booked them on the spot. The song they were playing, "The Look of Love," brought the tempo of the big tent right to where it should be, now that the meal had been eaten and the toasts had been given. Wedding guests were on their feet and in each other's arms.

From across the room, Mac Carlton, the film producer, watched the waitress from the *Vanity Fair* party make her way around the room. As memorable as winning his first Oscar had been that night, she had left a bigger impression. Try as he might, from that night on, he couldn't get her out of his mind.

Of course, now he knew her name, and he'd followed her meteoric success: Tally Jones, prime-time television star and first-time Emmy nominee. He'd also seen those gossipy tidbits about her and the actor who had kissed her that night, Gabriel McNamara, a B-list television actor who had more media savvy than talent.

But McNamara wasn't here now. And if the tabloids were to be believed, it was over between the two of them. It was time for Mac finally to introduce himself, and this time, he planned on succeeding in that task.

Intent on asking her to dance, he was halfway across the room when he felt Josh slapping him on the back. He smiled genially at the groom; congratulated him on his beautiful bride; passed on Josh's offer to be introduced to the porn star Taylor Made, who seemed to have captured the attention of every guy in the room over seventeen and under seventy (possibly a few over that age, too); and tried to bring the conversation around to Tally Jones by complimenting Josh on recognizing her talent and placing her on the fast track. By the time he'd gotten Josh caught up on his new project—he was in preproduction on *Cloistered*, a film that was to start shooting soon on location in Paris, with Jean-Claude Dumont directing—the beautiful Tally Jones was nowhere to be found.

He finally spotted her, outside on the terrace overlooking the cliffs and the ocean below. It was dark outside, but her silver dress shimmered in the soft light of the full moon. The wind had kicked up, and the gusts made her long skirt sway like a bell.

Mac had made it out of the tent and was just about to stroll over when he saw someone came out of the shadows and approach her. She didn't see the man at first, because she was looking out to sea. To get her attention, the man nuzzled her neck. Mac recognized him immediately, even in profile: McNamara.

She looked up at him, and although Mac couldn't see her face, he could tell by the way her body stiffened that she was fighting the impulse to embrace him. When a second later she gave in and fell into McNamara's arms, Mac knew it was game over, even before he'd had a chance to suit up.

He left before Josh and Sadie cut the cake. The next day was Monday, and he and Dumont had a long day ahead of them. Although their film was to start shooting next month, they were still playing musical chairs with their leads, and he needed to be well rested and sharp. At least, that was the excuse he told himself as he headed home alone.

"I guess I'm too late," Gabriel murmured into Tally's ear just when she thought she'd put him out of her mind for the evening.

But there he was, right next to her, asking her forgiveness. He swore up and down that the girl from the hot tub had just been a one-night stand and that he regretted that he hadn't chased after Tally when she stalked out that night.

Looking into her eyes, he told her that he couldn't stand being apart from her another moment. "Please, Tally. Forgive me. It was stupid. I know that now. But that's no reason to hate me forever." He reached to stroke the back of her neck, and when she felt his hand there, she did exactly what she'd done the first time they met: gave in to him.

Chapter 18

BY THE FOLLOWING week, they were the golden couple again: Tally and Gabriel, rising from their limo together and walking, hand in hand, down the red carpet in front of the Nokia Theatre at the Emmys. The clicks of the cameras were accompanied by the shouts to look here, there, everywhere. Tally looked fantastic in her red form-fitting Dolce & Gabbana with a plunging backline, her hair upswept in an elegant chignon. It was a great night—*her* night—but she kept Gabriel front and center with her the entire time.

Once inside, the drinks kept coming. She could feel herself getting tipsy, and she enjoyed every second of the show—even when her category was announced and she didn't win after all. When the cameras panned to her to catch her reaction, Gabriel kissed her long and hard.

Eventually, Gabriel wandered off to mingle with the celebrated crowd, which was OK with her, because she wanted to schmooze, too. Right after the ceremony, they'd meet up and head over to the Governors Ball, before slipping out to the HBO party and finally winding up at the *Entertainment Tonight/People* party—at least, that's the way she imagined the evening would go.

As she walked through the crowd that had gathered backstage in the *Architectural Digest* green room, the name of her financial manager—Tanner Bascom—could be heard in anxious whispers making their way through the room. She tapped another of Steve's clients on the shoulder—one of the actors from *Brothers & Sisters*—then gave him a hug. "What were you saying about Tanner? Is everything all right?"

The guy winced. "Hardly. At least, not if you're one of his clients, and unfortunately, I fall into that category. Seems I've been scammed. And, as it turns out, I'm not the only one. He was arrested earlier today for securities fraud."

She grabbed him by the arm. "No! Tell me you're kidding, please!"

He shook his head. Watching the color drain from her face, he added, "Call your attorney tomorrow.

Probably a third of the people in this room got taken for something, so the line of creditors will be long—if there's anything left to recover."

Her savings. Her new house and its big fat mortgage. All of it had been managed by Tanner. Suddenly, the best day of her life became the worst. She stumbled out of the green room, looking for Gabriel, and found him flirting with one of the professional dancers from *Dancing with the Stars*.

She tugged on his tux sleeve. "We've got to leave, now!"

Gabriel smirked down on her. "Look, it's just a little harmless flirting. Nothing to get upset over—"

"No, Gabriel, you don't understand: *I'm broke.* Tanner Bascom is in jail for embezzling! The place is buzzing about it."

Gabriel's smile disappeared like a ghost in fog. Immediately, he grabbed his cell phone, but whatever number he punched rolled to voice mail. He slammed his fist on the bar in frustration. "Aw, hell! That son of a bitch!"

The party was definitely over.

"Damn it, Steve. I want some answers, now!" Tally glared at her manager from across the booth at the Polo Lounge. Josh, whom she'd asked to accompany her there as backup, sat silently, ready to jump in should she need help while firing Steve. The Tanner Bascom fiasco was the final straw.

The confident gaze that had always been Steve's hallmark was nowhere to be seen. In its place was defeat. He had fucked up royally, and he knew it.

"Tally, I don't know what to say. He fooled me, too. He fooled *everyone*." Steve looked down into the depths of his wine glass, as if he'd find the answers he needed there.

Tally teared up. "Listen, Steve, just level with me. What do I have left?"

"Not much, I'm afraid. I thought I was doing you a favor when I asked Burt Tillman to front-load the deal Josh made for you. Although you've still got three more episodes to film, unfortunately, you've been paid in advance for them."

In other words, Tally really was broke.

Josh shoved his silverware to the side and leaned forward on his elbows. "Thus far, accounting forensics shows that Tanner has not made a payment on your mortgage since you moved in," he said quietly.

Tally slumped back into her seat. "So I'm a deadbeat who can get locked out of my home at any time. Just . . . great."

Steve stood up. "Look, Tally, I know this is the end of the line for us. And I don't blame you. Just know that— Well, that working with you meant more to me than you'll ever know."

She nodded to him, but she didn't put out her hand to shake good-bye. She knew he'd want a kiss, anyway.

As Steve made his way out of the dining room, Tally turned to Josh. "I need to take on another project. Is there any feature stuff out there that still hasn't been cast?"

Josh shrugged. "Sorry, kiddo. If you're looking for something that shoots while you're on hiatus from *Dana Point,* most productions are locked and loaded already." His head tilted to one side. "Wait a minute, I just thought of something. I was talking to the producer of Jean-Claude Dumont's upcoming feature—it's an indie—and he mentioned they were still rounding out the cast. In fact, he hasn't filled the role of the female lead. It starts shooting in Paris next month, around the time you should be wrapping your show for the season."

"Wow! It would be a dream to work with Dumont. Will he allow me to audition?"

"Hell, I don't think you'll have to. The producer was pretty sold on you already. Let me call him up and see if they'll bite." He gulped down the rest of his martini, then added, "I'm guessing it's going to be rough on you to be away from Gabriel for the ten or so weeks of the film shoot."

She clicked her glass to his. "Well, we'll find out, won't we?"

"Dumont, eh?" Gabriel shrugged. It wasn't exactly the reaction she expected from him. "Why don't you ask Josh to look for something shooting here?"

She turned over on the bed to face him. "I did. But I think it would be an honor to work with Dumont. And I certainly don't mind working in Paris."

"Yeah, I'll just bet you don't." He pulled her closer to him. "With your French director."

I've never made him jealous before, she thought. *Maybe that's the key to his heart.*

It wasn't. As she turned to kiss him, he avoided her mouth. Instead, he flipped her onto her stomach and thrust into her with such savagery that she begged him to stop.

He did, and then he turned his back to her.

She picked up her clothes and left his house without a word.

Chapter 19

For Tally, working on *Cloistered* was a dream come true.

She loved Paris. She enjoyed walking among the women in their sleek jeans, elegant blouses, and scarves. The street markets were laden with wonderful foods, antiques, and art. Apartment buildings were adorned with French doors that led out to wrought-iron terraces cascading with colorful flowers. The mansard roofs were topped with eye-catching gargoyles and angels. Cafés, bookstores, and boutiques filled in the picturesque neoclassical buildings on wide tree-lined avenues, making up the *arrondissements* that fanned out from the River Seine.

She also loved the script. In the film, she played

Emma, a former nun drawn into deadly intrigue based on her knowledge of a priest's murder. Tally recognized immediately how fortunate she was that, in the right directional hands, the role would allow her to leave her mark on the screen. Plus, the two male leads already signed—an older French actor and a young Shakespearean-trained British star—were both veterans of the indie scene and well respected by the international film community.

The first week, their scenes were all shot on a quaint Parisian side street, where a crowd gathered every day to watch. One man was constantly present. In his late thirties, adorably cute albeit scruffy, with a three-day beard and a rumpled jacket, he'd sit at a café across the street, an espresso in front of him, along with a cell phone and a copy of the *International Herald Tribune*.

Very French, thought Tally. *And he watches our takes with such intensity.*

Unfortunately, she was less enthralled with Jean-Claude Dumont, her temperamental director, who was take-crazy and always changing *Cloistered*'s script on a whim. On day six, when Dumont insisted that a difficult scene in which Tally had to be slapped by her costar be shot over and over, the mysterious man made his way over to the set. Although she didn't know French, his heated discussion with Dumont, in which her name was mentioned, left little doubt that he was just as upset with the director's treatment of her as she was. Already emotionally drained, Tally stared listlessly as the two men continued arguing until Dumont glared at her and stalked off.

"Come on, let's get out of here," the stranger said to her. His perfect English astonished her, and it took her a moment to realize that he'd taken her hand and was leading her away from the set.

Wondering what the hell was happening and if her paycheck had just gone up in smoke, she followed. The rest of the cast and crew seemed just as lost, but when the stranger snapped his fingers at them, the crew began the arduous process of packing up the set.

Dumont had been complaining daily about France's film workers union, and it occurred to Tally that the guy might be the local union boss. Under that very possible presumption, she pulled away from him. "What did you just say to Jean-Claude? Did you just get me fired?"

"Seriously, Miss Jones, you've got nothing to worry about. As far as I'm concerned, it's your movie, not Dumont's. His foolishness was nothing more than a series of selfish indulgences—"

"What do you mean, 'as far as you're concerned'? Who the hell are you, anyway?"

He broke out into a surprised laugh. "Let's just say I'm you're biggest fan."

Oh, great, just what I need. A union boss who's also a stalker, Tally thought.

When she started to walk off again, he grabbed her wrist. "Hey, Tally, not so fast—"

"Let go of me!" At times like this, the S&M maneuvers Mandy had taught her for putting a guy in his place paid off handsomely. A quick kick to the groin had him doubled over a moment later.

When he gasped out, "I'm the producer of *Cloistered,*" she stopped midway through her second kick.

Oops. So, the rumpled hunk was Mac Carlton, the renowned independent producer.

Tally thought back to the pictures she had seen of him in *Variety,* Page Six, and *The Hollywood Reporter,* in which he was always clean-shaven, with his neatly trimmed hair combed into place, usually in black tie while walking the red carpet with the latest, greatest supermodel or celebutante on his arm.

While his taste in women was certainly A-list, Tally was more impressed with his track record as a producer. Like this film, most of Carlton's projects were known to keep audiences on the edges of their seats and to win over critics while also doing well at the box office, garnering decent numbers, if not blockbuster.

Thinking she'd blown this opportunity, she stammered, "M-Mr. C-Carlton, please forgive me! I didn't know who you were. I am so, so sorry—"

Slowly, Mac rose to his feet, but he remained slightly bent over. He smiled wanly. "If I'm not an invalid for life, I'm sure I can think of a way you can make it up to me."

"I insist. Let me take you out to dinner. Please."

"It's a deal. I'll pick you up at seven."

He showed up right on time at the cozy little flat that had been rented for her on the Left Bank. Tally invited him in and told him she had a surprise waiting for him: she had made them dinner.

The apartment had a small but adequate galley kitchen and a great view of the Seine. The meal she prepared was simple: roasted chicken in wine sauce, sauteed vegetables, a fresh baguette, and, of course, a lovely French wine. She'd found the local ingredients at the closest outdoor market and picked up a few dessert tarts from the corner bakery as well.

Throughout dinner, they talked shop. He asked her how she felt the shoot had been going overall and informed her that he had heard Dumont was abusive from a few members in the cast. Dumont's treatment of her had put the final nail in the coffin.

Tally picked at her food while she tried to get up

the courage to ask the question foremost in her mind. Finally, she took a deep breath and said, "Now that Dumont has been fired, will the film be abandoned?"

"Heck, no." Mac took a generous bite of his *coq au vin*. "In fact, I've already put out feelers to Kent Whitman. I'd considered him initially for the project, but at the time, he had a scheduling conflict. Turns out he's free now, and we should know something soon." He smiled at her. "If you don't mind hanging tight for a day or two until all of this gets ironed out, we might just pull off a miracle."

He spent the rest of the evening talking about his hopes for the film and answering all of the questions she threw his way. She hadn't realized he was the son of the actress Elizabeth Carlton and that his father, Richard, was the head of Royalton Studios.

"My show, *Dana Point*, is shot on Royalton's lot," she informed him.

"I know. I've seen you there." He colored somewhat. "In fact, I suggested to Jean-Claude that you'd be perfect for the role of Emma."

So, Mac Carlton really *was* her biggest fan!

He continued, "I have my production offices at Royalton, too. For the first time since I became a producer, I'm working on a project with my father. After I left the company to do my own thing, we didn't see each other for years. He was angry with me, but it was either that or keep making his kind of movies instead of mine. He's a stubborn dictator, and he wouldn't even discuss funding my films, let alone offer a distribution deal, so my last six movies were handled by Fine Line." Mac took a sip of his wine. "That's OK. I didn't mind having to prove to him that I was a good bet. Like me, he flipped over the script for *Cloistered,* and I was shocked when Dad called me to suggest that we take a meeting for it."

What Mac didn't say to Tally was that Richard Carlton wasn't too happy with his choice for the role of Emma. Richard thought she was too fresh. Yes, he was perfectly justified in saying so, given that Tally had yet to prove she could carry a film, but Mac would enjoy proving his father wrong.

He dug into his dessert. "I can't believe you spent the entire afternoon cooking for me. It's the first home-cooked meal I've had in quite some time."

She laughed. "Since I've been so busy with my career, I haven't had time to do any cooking lately in LA. For me, it's fun and relaxing. And besides, it just feels like the right thing to do, here in Paris."

"Ha! Usually, when I'm with a woman in Paris, the very *last* thing she's thinking about doing is spending time in the kitchen." He leaned back. "In fact, I'm not sure the most recent woman in my life could find the kitchen in her house if she used a GPS."

So that he couldn't see her blush, Tally busied herself picking up the dirty dishes. "With this break in the shooting, will she be joining you here?"

Mac laughed raucously. "I hope not! I'm flying solo these days."

Discovering that Mac Carlton was unattached made Tally smile, and she blushed even deeper.

Because Mac was so convinced that Tally would be great in his film, she started believing it herself, and it showed in the daily rushes.

At night, she and Mac usually joined the new director, Kent Whitman, and the other members of the cast for dinner. Tally noticed that Mac always found a way to be seated beside her, and on her few days off, he insisted on showing her around Paris.

"Seriously, don't feel as if you have to babysit the talent," she said, smiling.

He laughed. "Is that your way of telling me that you don't want to spend time with me?"

"On the contrary! You're wonderful company."

In fact, he was too wonderful. It would have been so easy to fall in love with him, but she held back. After all, there was still the business of *Cloistered* to finish up.

Her relationship with Gabriel was unfinished business, too.

One Sunday, while Tally and Mac were window-shopping on the Left Bank, she noticed a man across the street taking pictures of them. By the next evening, those pictures and others of the two of them enjoying the city—and each other—appeared in the French celebrity magazine *Voici*.

"This is a disaster," Tally moaned when she saw the magazine as she and Mac walked by a newsstand during a stroll that evening. "We aren't having an affair! And I want to be known for my acting, not my supposed lovers."

Mac laughed uneasily, trying to make light of the situation. "At least we're getting some advance publicity for the film, right?" Seeing her frown, he added, "What's wrong? Are you afraid to be seen with me in public?"

Tally shook her head. The last thing she wanted to tell him was that she was wondering if Gabriel would see the same photo in *Us Weekly*. Instead, she said, "I guess all of this paparazzi stuff is still so new to me. It must be hard for you, having grown up in the spotlight. What's it like to have a father who is so powerful in Hollywood and a mother who is a famous movie star?"

Mac looked away for a moment before answering. "I wish I could tell you that we were one big happy family, but that would be a lie. My guess is that my parents' marriage was one of convenience."

Noting the puzzled look on Tally's face, he explained further. "It was the waning days of the studio system. Father was vice president in charge of production at Royalton when they met, and Mother was one of the last starlets to be put under contract there. She had just come off a successful Broadway debut. According to legend, she also had a offer from MGM, but Father's proposal cinched the deal for Royalton." Mac shrugged. "Unfortunately, he knocked her up immediately. She was just twenty-five, but she was still playing college coeds. The studio released her from *Say It Isn't True* because I was the cause of some pretty bad bouts of morning sickness. Father had effectively sidelined one of Royalton's most important assets. To this day, he still claims that almost killed both of their careers. Being a good Catholic girl, she was mortified at his suggestion that she find a way to 'take care of their little mistake.' I've had to prove him wrong every day of my life." Mac's tone was flippant, but the hurt on his face offered a truer reflection of his feelings.

Tally smiled uncertainly and said, "All's well that ends well, right? She came back and starred in some wonderful movies, and he ended up as head of the studio."

"Yes, by a cruel twist of fate. His predecessor had a fatal heart attack, and Father convinced Royalton's largest stockholders that he was the logical replacement." Mac smiled derisively. "He's been currying their favor ever since. As for Mother, I'm proud of her films, and I think she is, too. But for her sake, I wish there had been more of them."

"Why weren't there?"

Mac held Tally's gaze with his own. "No matter how talented she was, she was still the boss's wife. I think she got tired of the studio politics and the accusations of nepotism from the other actresses on the lot, so she retired." He paused and looked down. "And I'm sure it hurt her to hear the gossip about his affairs. Once she walked in on him unannounced and caught him red-handed."

Tally flinched. She couldn't help thinking that maybe he knew more about her and Gabriel than he was letting on.

The night of the wrap party was bittersweet for Tally. As much as she missed Los Angeles, she had come to love Paris so much, not to mention the joy of seeing Mac every day, and she wondered what would happen when they got back to Hollywood.

As he walked her from the wrap party to her apartment, he whispered in her ear, "Before we leave, I owe you a home-cooked dinner. Care to join me at my hotel tomorrow night, eight o'clock? I'm staying at the George Cinq."

Tally's stomach did a flip. They no longer had the pretense of business as usual or babysitting the talent. Besides, his tone made it clear that this had nothing to do with business.

The next day, when she got to his hotel, she was directed to the eighth floor. She was surprised to find that Mac's room wasn't the usual businessman's accommodation but a sumptuously appointed suite. Gold brocade drapes flowed to the floor, the cream-colored walls had crown and picture-frame molding, the furnishings were ornate Louis XIV antiques, and paintings from the same period adorned the walls.

Tally gave a low whistle. "Wow, this is some bachelor pad."

"Actually, it's the honeymoon suite." He pulled the drapes. Beyond the large French doors was a straight-on view of the Eiffel Tower.

Tally turned to him. "Forget acting. I should be a producer instead!"

Mac laughed. "Well, there's got to be a few perks that come with the job, right? I do have to put up with the talent."

He led her to the small dining table by the window.

When he pulled off the silver dome that had been covering a tray, she found three chocolate-covered strawberries. Next to the plate, a bottle of Dom Pérignon White Gold Jeroboam was being iced in a sterling silver cooler.

It was her turn to laugh. "What, dessert first?"

"This is just the first course. The best is yet to come." He offered no further explanation of what was to come. His adoring gaze said it all.

She didn't mind when he wrapped his arms around her waist or when he gently kissed the back of her neck. And she didn't hesitate at all as he pulled her into the bedroom, where the king bed with its diamond-patterned duvet and large feather pillows awaited them.

He insisted on undressing her himself. He did so slowly, one garment at a time. As each part was revealed—a creamy white shoulder, the crook of an arm, a nipple—his eyes lingered on the magnificence of her body, as if he were examining the *Venus de Milo*.

She'd never been with a man who made love so gently, who took his time to make her happy. His caresses tickled her like velveteen. His tongue teased every nook and cranny, leaving her damp with anticipation, moaning for him to satisfy her, which he did as he plunged into the vortex of her very being. When she cried out, it was only because pain and pleasure overcame her so completely, to her great delight.

He was not selfish. Instead, he waited until he heard her sigh with pleasure before pulling her on top of him. As she mounted him, she squeezed him tightly. His gasp told her that he, too, was ready to come beside her. She drew his hand to her mouth and encircled his thumb lovingly with her lush lips. This brought him to a climax, just as she, too, was racked with ecstasy.

Their night of lovemaking was long but not long enough for all she wanted to do to him. And what she wanted him to do to her.

As the first rays of a new day streamed in through the French doors, he wrapped her in one of the hotel's big fluffy robes and carried her out to the terrace to watch the sun rise over the Eiffel Tower. Maybe they should have seen the paparazzi on the street below them, but they didn't. They were too wrapped up in seeing Paris awaken through each other's eyes.

At the airport the next day, while they were waiting at their gate to catch the flight home, Tally noticed the latest cover of *Voici*. It was a photo of her and Mac, on the terrace in their robes, kissing.

Tally's face turned crimson. For the first time in

two days, she thought of Gabriel, and suddenly, she couldn't breathe. Would the photos have made it to the American tabloids as well?

As they boarded the plane, she avoided Mac's eyes. Once seated, she pretended to be reading the first *Dana Point* script of the new season, which had been couriered to her apartment on the last day of shooting. They were over the Atlantic when, finally, Mac leaned in for a kiss. "You've been awfully quiet. Is the script that great? Tally, what's up?"

You really don't want to know. Or do you? She turned to look him straight in the eye, and when she finally answered, her tone was blunt. "What happens now?"

"Whatever you want. You know, if this movie is as good as I think it is, you have a wonderful career ahead of you. And one thing I've learned in this industry is that everything is on the table for negotiation."

He thinks he's being cute, she thought. But it wasn't what she wanted to hear from him. "No, I mean what happens with *us?*"

He put down the folder of financial statements he'd been reviewing. "Why don't you tell me what you want?"

What do you think *I want? And don't you want it, too? Obviously not,* she thought. Tally turned toward the window so that he couldn't see the tears in her eyes.

Seeing the emotions play out on her face, he shrugged and muttered, "Look, no pressure, OK? I guess what I'm trying to say, Tally is that I hope we stay friends."

Friends. As in fuck buddies. So, this is it, she thought. *I've just had a Paris fling with the producer of my movie. What an idiot I am!*

Except for a few curt answers to his idle chitchat, she was silent for most of the long flight home. She even pretended to sleep part of the way. Why not? She had nothing else to say to him, except *au revoir, mon ami.*

When the plane landed at LAX, she let him get up and out of his seat first. As passengers queued up and jostled to be next in line on the jetway, she fiddled with her bag in the overhead compartment so that others would get between them. He'd either wait for her in the boarding lounge or just take off—she didn't care which.

What she didn't expect was for Gabriel to be waiting for her on the other side of customs. In fact, she didn't even see him until he was right in front of her. On his face was the grin that melted millions of women's hearts each week, and in his arms was a bouquet of roses that got crushed between them as he swept her up into his arms and kissed her hungrily.

When he let her go, she glanced around. Where was Mac?

Then she saw him over Gabriel's shoulder. The look on his face went from shock to anger to derision. But he didn't say a word.

He didn't pull Gabriel off her, either. In fact, he did absolutely nothing except shrug and walk away.

She wanted to run to him, to ask him if their tryst in Paris had meant anything at all to him, but Gabriel draped his arm over her shoulders, holding her firmly. "God, I can't wait to get you home. We've got a lot of catching up to do."

She tore her eyes away from Mac's back for just a second to nod and smile in reply. By the time she looked up again, Mac was gone.

As Mac got into the town car that was waiting for him outside of baggage claim, he was fuming. He climbed into the backseat and slammed the door. *So, she's still in love with him,* he thought. *I was just a diversion during the shoot.* No wonder she freaked out when she saw the photos of them in that magazine. And that kiss-off on the plane! First the tears, then the ice princess routine. *I can't believe I just let her off the hook with that "friends" line. I'm such a jerk.*

For a split second, he wondered what she would have done if he'd just laid it all out on the line, if he had told her how he'd loved her since the first moment he saw her and how the thought of her going back to Gabriel would break his heart.

Because that was exactly what was happening.

Well, now he knew what her response would have been. She would have felt sorry for him. And he didn't need her pity. He needed a stiff drink.

Chapter 20

IT WAS AS though nothing had changed between them. Gabriel began calling the shots as soon as they left the airport. He wouldn't even let her go back to her place first—apparently, he had something else in store.

"Please, Gabriel, I'm so tired. I want to shower, check my mail—"

"Aw, but I've got so many surprises waiting for you. And you know we can bathe together at my house." He drove straight to the Pacific Coast Highway, then north to Malibu, to his pigsty.

By the time they got to his house, she had made up her mind to call a taxi immediately to take her home. She wasn't going to be his willing playmate anymore.

But Gabriel had other plans in mind. This became blatantly clear the moment he closed the door behind her—and locked it. Then he leaned in over her, jerked her head up by pulling her hair, and forced her lips open with his own. Her terrified gasps did nothing to stop him. When she tried hitting him with her fist, he grabbed both her wrists and held them behind her back.

"Does your new boyfriend know you like it rough?" Gabriel hissed.

When she didn't respond, he yanked her blouse open. The buttons popped off and rolled on the floor. His hands felt dirty on her body, and she longed for Mac's tenderness.

Gabriel pulled her toward the armchair facing the big picture window. "Remember doing it right here for the first time, babe? I left out one thing that time."

From the drawer on the side table that sat nearby, he pulled out two wrist straps. He positioned her so that she was bent over the chair, and with a snap, he tethered a wrist to one arm of the chair, then her second wrist to the other. He unzipped her skirt so that it fell to her feet and yanked off her panties. He left her heels on.

"Please, Gabriel, untie me! I'm not comfortable standing like this!"

"Aw, that's too bad, Tally. *But I really don't care.*"

She had her back to him, but she could still see the room reflected in the picture window. He disappeared for a moment.

Where has he gone? What's he getting? Horror swept through her. She yanked at both shackles, but neither of them gave even a millimeter. In fact, they seemed to get tighter with each pull.

"Why? Why don't you care? I thought you loved me!" she cried out frantically, but she didn't know where he was or if he could even hear her.

Suddenly, she heard him rummaging in his messy kitchen. When she looked up again, she saw his reflection in the window.

The honey bears.

His hands were loaded with the small plastic containers. He lined them up on the windowsill in front of her; there were six of them. Then, very slowly, as if performing some sad, sick ritual, he unscrewed the cap on the one farthest to the right and approached her with it. "Admit it, sweet thing, it was never really love between us. Just sex."

He dripped the honey onto her back. She could feel it roll slowly down her spine, to the top of her rear. He followed it with his tongue, lapping lazily all the way down her back. When he got to the base of her spine, he stopped and smeared her rump with the sticky liquid.

She shuddered, but that only made him laugh. "I've wanted to do this to you from day one. Remember the first time you came here, when you asked me why I had all the bear honey containers? I figured, 'Tally's a sweet kid. Sure, my bondage partners love it. My hookers tolerate it. But this would be *way* too kinky for her.' Besides, I didn't want to lose a high-profile arm charm like you. So I made up the bullshit about collecting them for my niece. I don't have a niece! I don't even have siblings. Jeez, Tally, you didn't even bother to Google me. What kind of girlfriend does that make you?"

He laughed raucously, then made his way back to the windowsill and picked up another honey bear. This time, though, he poured a glob of honey onto the palm of his hand. He leaned down and grabbed one of her breasts, smearing it generously with the sticky goo, then started sucking on it hard. She recoiled, and when he came up for air, she had to turn her head so that she wouldn't throw up at the sight of his face smeared with honey.

He went back to the window for another bear. He chuckled as he unscrewed it and held it up to the light. "I'm guessing this is nothing compared to what Mac Carlton did to you. I'll bet he has his own kinks and fetishes. And I bet he had plenty of time to show you all of them. Well, now it's my turn."

He poured the thick amber liquid into the palm of his hand, then moved behind her. When she heard him unzipping his pants, she closed her eyes and shook her head.

With one hand, he spread the honey between her legs, pushing them so far apart that her head went deep into the cushion of the chair as she straddled it. With the other, he smeared the honey onto his cock. She could hear him groan as it grew in his fist. Then he plunged it into her, deep to her core, again and again.

She cried out. Not in ecstasy or even in pain, but in shame and disgust.

Finally, he was spent. Afterward, for what felt like a very long time, he lay draped over her, his cheek resting against her shoulder blade. "Just so you never forget who owns you," he whispered maliciously.

Eventually, he lifted himself up. "Time flies when you're having fun, but I've got to leave you, Tal. I'm having drinks with that new actress they've just hired on *The Office*. She's a cutie, isn't she? Aw, what the hell, let her wait. Sex with you is always so *sweet*." He walked to the window for another honey bear.

No, Tally thought. *Not again. Never again.*

The chair was heavy, but when she placed one knee in the center of its back, she found she could raise it, with both hands strapped to its arms.

As Gabriel applied honey to himself with his back toward her, she pulled the chair straight up into the air, then smacked him over the head with it. The thump was painfully loud, and when he crumpled to the floor, she saw the bruise on his forehead already forming.

The pressure of the blow was too hard for one arm of the chair to withstand, and it broke away from the seat, allowing Tally to disentangle her arm from it. She dragged the chair to the fireplace, and with the fire poker, she levered the other arm away from the chair until it let loose, too.

Finally free, she grabbed her cell phone and arranged for a cab to meet her at the Malibu Ranch Market up the street. She wanted lots of people around her, in case Gabriel came after her again.

She walked over to his kitchen sink and frantically scrubbed the honey off her hands, face, and chest before slipping back into her skirt and panties. Without buttons, all she could do was tie her blouse at the waist and button her jacket all the way up.

Then, feeling sticky, dirty, and shameful, she ran out.

The taxi was already at the market when she got there. By then, she'd made up her mind. "Take me to Pacific Palisades, please."

The driver nodded and began heading in the direction of Mac's house.

At first, Mac was reluctant to let her enter. His ego was hurt.

"I made a mistake," she said softly.

He thought about the first time he'd seen her and all the wide-eyed innocence she'd had that night at the Sunset Tower. Now her innocence was gone. Did Gabriel McNamara have anything to do with that?

Gently, he took Tally into his arms. When she began to sob, he said nothing and just held her even closer. When she stopped, he said, "Tell me what he did to you."

Still in tears, with her head buried in his neck, she told him what happened. Afterward, he cradled her in his arms and took her up to his bedroom. While she lay in his bed, her ran her a bath.

As she sat in the big warm tub with the view of the PCH and the beach and ocean beyond, he made a few calls. When she came out of the bathroom in his robe, her skin beneath it was clean and rosy. Still, he knew she'd be stained by the memory for a long, long time.

The fix was simple. Mac had called in a favor from an old pal, the producer of *Intensive Care*.

Like that of every actor, Gabriel McNamara's contract included a morals clause. Rape was immoral—and illegal. Gabriel wouldn't want to be accused of that. Nor would he want to do time for it. He was too pretty.

There were probably enough women who had gotten the honey rape treatment from the asshole that at least some of them would be willing to talk about it, a fact that Mac pointed out to the show's producers. Of course, they agreed with him on all counts. Besides, all actors were replaceable.

Later that week, when Tally read in *Variety* that Gabriel had been dropped from *Intensive Care*, the thought crossed her mind that Mac could have had something to do with it, but she decided it was just Gabriel's karma finally catching up with him.

Chapter 21

BLISS, FINALLY.

After so many ups and downs in her professional and personal life, Tally felt everything was falling into place. The fee she'd earned from *Cloistered* allowed her to pay off her house in full, and her home provided her with the peace of mind she felt she needed to survive in such a volatile industry.

Sadie and Mandy referred to the house as "Tally's dollhouse" because of its charm. And despite its meager furnishings and the fact that Tally hadn't yet unpacked most of her boxes, its central location—between Sadie's Malibu digs and Mandy's elegant new home in Pasadena—made it the perfect place for the three friends to meet and relax.

Actually, Sadie seemed just as excited as Tally about her new home. "I saw a wonderful knotty-pine table that would fit perfectly in your foyer. We should go look at it before someone else snaps it up," she urged her friend one day.

Tally sighed. "You know how crazy my schedule is, now that *Dana Point* is back in production. I'm on the set almost twelve hours a day." Watching Sadie's face realign itself into a look of disappointment, Tally immediately regretted her words. "I'm sorry, Sadie. I hope you didn't think I meant I didn't have time for you. It's just that things are so hectic these days—"

Sadie forced a smile. "Hey, no need for apologies. It's not you I'm upset with but myself. Ever since I quit ICA, I seem to have more time on my hands than I know what to do with. I mean, you can only take so many tennis lessons and attend so many yoga classes in any given week, right?"

Mandy looked up from her BlackBerry. "I love those cute little tennis skirts! I've got to remind Jerry that we haven't done a plot with a tennis pro yet. On second thought, maybe I should put it out there on my Taylor Made Facebook fan page first and see what kind of response the idea gets." Inspired, she began typing even more furiously.

Tally shook her head. Mandy's hard-core fans gave her feedback on everything: their favorite Taylor Made movies, her technique, her costars' equipment, and certainly her costumes—when she wore them.

She and Mandy were thriving in their acting careers, whereas Sadie's had ground to a halt from the moment she met Josh. And Sadie had left her fledgling agenting gig as soon as she got married. Now she seemed somewhat lost. Tally put her arm around her friend and tried to cheer her up. "Are you pleased with the guy who replaced you as Josh's assistant?" she asked.

Sadie shrugged. "Seth is OK. He's one of those bright-eyed, bushy-tailed go-getters."

Tally laughed. "Nothing wrong with that, right?"

"I guess not. It's just that . . ." She hesitated, as if contemplating the right way to say what was on her mind. "Well, I get the feeling that he'll say anything—and *do* anything—to get ahead. He's not looking out for Josh. He's looking out for himself."

Tally smiled. "Sadie, when it comes to Josh, no one will *ever* look out for him as much as you. He's a very lucky guy."

Sadie laughed. "Yeah, I guess I've done so well by him that I worked myself out of a job."

"Now you have the time—and the money—to go back to your acting lessons. You know Randall will always take you back," Tally said.

"Don't I know it." Sadie frowned. "He calls me up

at least once a week, but I feel like he's more interested in having a connection to Josh through me than in teaching me the skills I'd need to be a successful actress. I'm just now realizing the consequences of being Josh Gold's wife."

"Don't you mean the *opportunities*?" Tally said, trying to put a positive spin on the situation.

"Yeah, I guess it's all how you look at it. If it weren't for Josh, we wouldn't have gotten that beautiful venue for our wedding or a caterer who was willing to do it practically at cost just because she knew so many celebrities and stars were going to attend."

Mandy chimed in. "I swear, Sadie, that was the most beautiful wedding I've ever attended. Maybe you should plan weddings."

Sadie nodded thoughtfully. "Frankly, *it was* a lot of fun. And I enjoyed the challenge."

Tally looked around her empty living room. "Speaking of challenges, just because I don't have time to find some furniture doesn't mean you can't be a pal and scout out some good pieces for me. In fact, I know your taste well enough to give you carte blanche—within my budget, of course."

Sadie brightened. "OK, you're on. But now that you no longer have to worry about making house payments, I'm going to hit you up for a *real* decorating budget."

∽

In addition to having her very own dollhouse, Tally had another reason to be happy: Mac truly loved her, and she knew it. Not just because he told her so, repeatedly. More important to Tally—particularly after her volatile relationship with Gabriel—was that he *showed* his love for her in so many ways. Like the way he asked her opinion on whether they should go out to eat or hike or just hang out at home. Since Tally now had a face recognized by millions of people, he let her choose how public they should be.

"I grew up with a famous mother," he reminded her. "I remember how annoying it was to have people come up to you all the time, no matter where you were or what you were doing. Only Mother was never as sweet with her fans as you."

Tally appreciated his understanding. Unlike Gabriel, she preferred places that didn't light up on the paparazzis' radar screens, so they usually ended up in little out-of-the-way places where the food was great and they would be left alone.

Mac's love also showed up in many random acts of kindness. Once, when she had to cancel their lunch date because her scenes were running late, he had a picnic basket delivered to her trailer. And he always stuck around the lot until she was done with the day's filming, just so they could ride home together.

Best of all was the way he made love to her. No, *with* her. Slowly, as if he had all the time in the world to please her. He loved to hear her gasp with pleasure, to watch her back arch in anticipation to his touch, and to hear her sigh in his ear, "I love you, too, Mac." And, unlike Gabriel, he never left her alone after sex.

Sometimes she wondered if his love for her clouded his judgment of her acting skills, but he almost fell out of his chair laughing when she brought it up. "If you're pulling the wool over my eyes, then I'm not the only one. You auditioned for Burt Tillman, remember? He's a pretty hard nut to crack. And aren't you the same Tally Jones who was nominated for an Emmy in her very first season on television?" Then he got serious. "Besides, movies are big business. I can't afford to let my heart get in the way of other people's money, not to mention my own investment of cash and sweat equity."

In fact, Mac was very excited about what he was seeing in the postproduction process on *Cloistered*. Kent Whitman's directorial work melded seamlessly with the footage shot previously by the temperamental Dumont, thanks to the first-rate editor Mac had hired on his new director's recommendation.

Whenever she got done shooting *Dana Point* early,

Tally made her way over to Mac's offices to view the raw edits of *Cloistered*. She loved learning how that portion of the filmmaking process was done and seeing how her first film was coming together. Mac got a kick out of her enthusiasm for it all. "Your performance, and that of the rest of the cast, is just one piece of movie magic," he explained one day when she stopped by. "It starts with a great script and insightful direction, but you also need truly artistic cinematography, editing, music, and sound effects to create what people like to call 'movie magic.'"

She gave him a kiss on the forehead. "You forgot the role of the producer."

Mac laughed. "We just find the money and land a distribution deal."

"I'd say that's pretty important." Tally's smile disappeared. "Seriously, Mac, thank you for believing in me and trusting me with your film."

"Don't sell yourself short, gorgeous. If I hadn't hired you, some other producer or director would have eventually caught on to what the rest of America seems to know: that Tally Jones is a superb actress who lights up the screen. I just beat everyone else to the punch."

Chapter 22

"I HATE THAT BITCH," Susie murmured through clenched teeth.

Garfield, who was gluing extensions onto her real hair, was the only person in the trailer able to hear her. Of course, that's just what Susie wanted, because Garfield was the biggest gossip monger on the set. Next to Ben Kendrick, of course, but Ben was already Tally's biggest cheerleader, so he was no use to Susie. Garfield also knew which side his bread was buttered on, however, and that's where his allegiance went.

"She's just a tart." Garfield sniffed. "And to think they considered honoring her with an Emmy! That's only because they didn't know *you'd* be coming back."

"Burt *begged* me." Susie paused to scrutinize the

extensions, then waved her tacit approval. "He cried like a baby in my arms. You *know* that."

"Absolutely." Like everyone else on the set, Garfield knew how much Burt really hated Susie. Sure, Susie had been a ratings draw during her first few seasons, but it was only when Tally had been hired that the ratings climb really started. But Garfield wasn't man enough to remind her of that. Besides, he preferred to dish. "She's had it too damn easy, that one. Who the hell does she think she is, sashaying in here and taking your place?"

Susie gave him a dirty look. "What do you mean, taking my place? She can't take my place if *I'm still here*."

"N-no," Garfield stuttered. "What I meant is that she's nothing more than a spoiled little brat. Just look at her! She's a nobody, and she has a great role on a hit TV show and a new movie coming out this fall with some hot buzz, thanks to the affair she's having with the movie's producer. Can you believe they actually hooked up in Paris? How *gauche*."

Susie nodded grudgingly. As long as Garfield had that hot glue jar in his hand, she wasn't going to chastise him. "Yeah, I saw the headlines. So she was sucking face to sweeten her paycheck. What's the big deal?"

"Oh, nothing . . . except that Tally the Tease

dumped that hunk Gabriel McNamara for him." He shuddered at the thought. "Talk about stupid. To top it off, just to clear the playing field, her new lover boy got Gabriel axed from his show—"

Susie sat straight up in the chair and in the process almost lost what was left of her real hair, which was tethered to Garfield's glue brush. "Whoa, whoa, whoa! Slow down. Who is this guy, and what did he do to Gabriel McNamara?"

Garfield smiled smugly. "Where have you been, doll, in a crypt?" Seeing Susie's reaction to his comment, Garfield suddenly realized that he'd overstepped the sacred boundary between star and minion. "This is *totally* between you and me." Garfield leaned in for the pièce de résistance, "but I heard it from the highest source that Mr. Suit got the goods on his competition and then tossed them to the producers at *Intensive Care.* They had no other choice but to let Gorgeous Gabe go."

"Ha." Susie leaned back into her chair. "That guy must have had some real dirt to throw around. And some real clout."

"Mac Carlton, my sweet, is Richard Carlton's son. Talk about the top of the food chain."

So little Tally Jones has wrangled herself one of Hollywood's top players, Susie thought. *But he doesn't swing the biggest dick on the lot. His daddy, Richard, does.*

She smiled as she remembered her mother's one golden rule about men: aim high, and don't miss.

I wonder how Tally will do with a little competition.

Garfield twirled her around to the mirror so that she could admire his handiwork. Of course, Susie loved what she saw.

She always did.

Richard Carlton loved it when people fawned all over him; it was one of the perks of being a studio head. When the stars who appeared in his movies and television shows kowtowed to him, talked to him with deference, and grew shy and awkward in his presence, he felt as if he owned the world. And in a very real sense, he owned *their* world—and they knew it, even if their fans couldn't recognize him to save their lives. That, too, was a reality of his position: power was a given, but fame was not.

He was always pleasantly surprised when one of his stars asked him for a private meeting. When this happened, he invariably instructed his assistant to say yes, but his hard and fast rule was that such a meeting was never to go beyond fifteen minutes—even if it was with someone as beautiful as Susie Sheppard, the diva on his network's biggest prime-time hit, *Dana Point.*

Susie entered his office as a vision in a low-cut-cream Armani suit, with a set of pearls, and her hair extensions hanging in coils below her shoulders. The effect was quite angelic. Ostensibly, she was there to ask him for a donation.

"It's for an orphanage in Mississippi. The poor children there have absolutely nothing! Even a small amount will go a long way," she purred.

How could he say no to her? The way she smiled at him as she looked deep into his eyes had him putting his pen to his checkbook with a flourish. He was conservative both in his business dealings and in his politics, and he couldn't stand it when actors used their fame to push some political cause, but charity—and for orphans, no less—that was a different story. And for Susie to take time from her lunch hour on the set to raise money for them, well, she really was an angel. It made him think twice about all those nasty rumors he'd heard about her over the past few years.

She thanked him profusely for his generosity, and as she leaned over his desk to get the check, her hand grazed his, just barely. He didn't pull back, and neither did she.

Interesting.

Susie segued the conversation to his son, Mac, and started going on about how proud he must be of his accomplishments, including that Oscar, and how the whole town was buzzing over Mac's newest project, *Cloistered*. Then she mentioned how lucky it was that the public had yet to learn the truth about the movie's lead, Tally Jones, a heavy cocaine user who had ducked out of rehab twice already.

Richard glared at Susie. "You seem to know a lot about Tally."

Susie arched an eyebrow. "She's my costar on *Dana Point*. When someone runs to the bathroom every hour and sniffles all day long . . . well, let's just put it this way, it's not hard to figure out their drug of choice. But don't take my word for it, ask Chase Bracken. Oh, but you can't. He got fired by Burt Tillman. Burt's got a little thing for Tally."

Richard shook his head. Although Tillman's shows made his network a lot of money, he'd never been too fond of the old drunk.

Susie did her best to look sympathetic. "I guess that's what happens when your producer becomes enamored with the talent, isn't it? Suddenly, the blinders go on. But you already know that, since the same thing has happened with Mac, too. His director, Jean-Claude Dumont, was having all that trouble with Tally on the set of *Cloistered*, then *he* got canned instead of her." Susie sighed. "I guess that's why Mac is working so hard to control the press around her. If anyone knew about her behavior, it could jeopardize all the money he and his investors have poured into the picture."

Investors like me, Richard thought. And if the film failed, Royalton's stockholders would be calling for Richard's head on a stake.

Susie slipped the check into her white silk Chanel clutch and snapped it shut. "But Royalton will survive. What's one more film in the red? The studio's television division carries the company anyway, right?"

Without waiting for his answer, Susie glided out the door.

Richard looked at his calendar. Mac was expected over to the house for dinner tonight. *Good,* he thought, *because my son has a lot of explaining to do.*

Chapter 23

"YOU LOOK BEAUTIFUL." Mac's eyes opened wide as they took her in. Tally was dressed in a fuchsia-colored strapless silk dress, and her hair was pulled back into a loose bun, revealing her beautiful long neck and the diamond strand earrings he'd given her the week before.

She did a slight bow, then took his hand as she maneuvered into the passenger seat of his Maserati GranCabrio. "Well, you said you had a surprise. I can't wait to find out where we're going."

He smiled, but that was it. He wasn't going to give anything away just yet.

He took the 110 out of Los Angeles toward Pasadena. "Let me guess," Tally said. "The Parkway Grill, right? No? Then it's got to be the Huntington—"

Mac laughed. "It's close to the hotel but not quite. Look, don't even try to guess, because you won't figure it out in a million years."

She realized why when they pulled up in front of the wrought-iron gates of a beautiful Italianate villa that looked as if it had been transported, stone by stone, from Tuscany. "Is this a private club? You must have to know someone to get in here!"

"No—and yes. But don't get too excited. The ambience might be the best thing about the night. Here's hoping that's not the case."

Mac punched in the security code, and the gates swung back silently. Italian cedars lined both sides of the driveway, which wound around for a hundred yards before reaching the estate's home itself. When they pulled up to the villa, the large double doors were opened by a butler, who walked briskly out to the car. Noting that there was someone in the passenger side, he made his way there first and helped Tally from the car. She waited while he opened the door for Mac.

The entry hall was circular and adorned with Impressionist paintings. The marble floors echoed at the tap of Tally's heels as she followed Mac down the wide hallway into a large paneled room that was obviously the living room. Three large, elegant white sofas created a conversation pit around a fireplace large enough for a man to stand up inside it. A huge painting of a hunt scene hung over the mantel, and the walls flanking the fireplace were lined from floor to ceiling with heavily molded bookcases. A Steinway grand piano took up one corner of the room, along with an antique harp. Another had a large round table as its centerpiece that was perfect for playing bridge.

Seated on one of the couches was Mac's mother, Elizabeth Hayden Carlton. Tally recognized her immediately from her pictures, but despite the elegance of her Escada ensemble and the expertly applied makeup, Mac's mother looked like a ghostly remnant of the vibrant actress she once was. It didn't help that her hair was dyed jet black, that her skeletal frame looked fragile, that her forehead was devoid of lines, and that her skin was stretched so tautly against her unnaturally high cheeks that it gave her a ghostly pallor.

Tally prayed that her own face did not reflect the disappointment in her eyes. Suddenly, she realized that Mac's decision to keep their destination a surprise had to do with his discomfort regarding his parents. Had he tried to prepare her for meeting them, she would have only been more nervous.

"The prodigal son returns," Elizabeth said with a touch of bitterness. Instead of standing to greet her son, she waved her crystal tumbler at him, sending a bit of its clear liquid spilling over the sides. "And who do we have here? Seems our Malcolm brought company home with him tonight, Richard."

My goodness, she's soused, Tally thought.

Out of the corner of her eye, the young actress noticed some movement by the huge bay window. Richard Carlton turned around to face them, and the smile on his face—which was, really, just a forced grimace—disappeared completely when he noticed Tally. In fact, he frowned and gulped down the last of his drink.

Obviously, Mac noticed this, too, because his voice had a false cheeriness Tally had never heard before when he said, "Mother, Father, I'd like to introduce you to Tally Jones. As you know, she's the star of *Cloistered.*"

The silence in the room was defeaning.

When Richard finally spoke, it was as if he were commenting on something unpleasant on the bottom of his shoe. "Yes, we know of Tally. Her reputation precedes her."

He didn't walk over to greet her or to shake her hand. Instead, he just glared at her.

Finally, Elizabeth rose uneasily from her perch on

the couch. "Well, this should be an interesting night. Shall we move into the dining room?"

Despite Mac's attempt to lighten the mood at dinner, nothing he could say warmed up the obvious chill that blanketed the room. Richard mustered all the politeness of someone who feels put upon to spend time with those he feels are beneath him, while Elizabeth, whose meal consisted of sucking on the olives that buoyed the many martini refills the butler poured generously into her Baccarat crystal tumbler, looked at Tally with pity.

Tally didn't know which was worse.

With the appearance of dessert, the scales tipped in Richard's favor. He had been ignoring Tally until then, but suddenly, he turned his attention to her. "Miss Jones, tell me, of all the wonderful actresses who grace our industry, how do you think you got the starring role in Mac's picture?"

The boldness of his question shocked her. Deciding that honesty was always the best policy, she said, "Well, Mr. Carlton, I was told by my agent, Josh Gold, that the director enjoyed my work on *Dana Point*. He found out I was available when the movie was scheduled to shoot, so he put in a call." She gave a little nervous laugh. "I guess you can say the rest is history."

"So, you didn't even audition?" Richard asked in mock wonder, then glanced at Mac. "How strange. I also find it curious that this very same director—one of the world's most revered directors, at that—was fired because of some altercation involving you."

"What are you trying to imply?" Mac jumped in. "I happened to be on the set when he was berating Tally. If you must know, it wasn't the first time Jean-Claude was abusive to the cast or crew."

The anger in Mac's voice made Tally cringe.

"And another thing," he continued. "It wasn't Jean-Claude's decision to hire Tally, it was mine."

Richard shot daggers at his son with his eyes. "I'm not surprised. It was a stupid mistake to hire an untried nobody with a scandalous reputation. Damn it, Mac, what were you thinking? I can't believe I let you talk me into putting Royalton's money on the line for—for *this*." He practically spit the words at Tally.

"What the hell are you talking about? Look, whatever you've read in the tabloids about Tally is just Hollywood gossip, complete and utter garbage! Hell, I can't believe you would take any of that stuff seriously—"

"For God's sake, she works at my studio! Don't you know I have people on the set whom I trust to tell me what I need to know about those who put our investments at risk?"

"You've got people spying on Tally?" Mac asked. Too angry to sit any longer, he stood up, rattling the glasses on the table with the force of his movement. Before he could lunge at his father, Tally grabbed his arm to hold him back. "I suppose you spy on me, too!"

"If I did, we wouldn't be having this conversation." Richard ran his hand through his steel-gray hair. "I would have known earlier about your plan to jeopardize the film."

"Granted, Tally wasn't on the short list," Mac conceded, though he was so angry the words were spoken through his teeth. "But Royalton's production chief approved Tally for the lead. In fact, they welcomed the choice. She's part of the Royalton family, and she's an Emmy nominee, for God's sake."

"And because you—and that old sod Burt Tillman—have done such a superb job in covering up for her, my studio will be out its investment in your film." Richard's rage showed in his shortness of breath. "I finally gave you a shot to bring it all home for Royalton—for *us*—and you blew it on some little tramp! Well, I hope she's good enough in bed that this was all worth it for you."

Mac, who had been clenching his napkin tightly, suddenly tossed it down on the table in anger. As it hit the table, Tally bolted straight up in her chair. *What on earth is going on? And what can Richard possibly think about me that would cause him to act this way?*

Calmly, Mac addressed his father. "Don't worry about Royalton's investment. I'll have it replaced by the close of business on Friday." With that, Mac grabbed Tally's hand and pulled her up out of her chair.

Mac didn't say one word on the drive out of Pasadena. When they arrived at his Pacific Palisades driveway, Tally found the nerve to ask, "Mac, won't replacing Royalton mean coming up with ten million dollars or so?"

He laughed derisively. "More like twenty, if you want the truth."

"But . . . where will you get that kind of money?"

"That's a very good question. Let's hope I find the answer to it before five o'clock Friday. Otherwise, I'll lose everything I've invested in *Cloistered,* and both of us can kiss our careers good-bye."

Chapter 24

"OK, DON'T OPEN your eyes until I tell you."

Tally nodded reluctantly but did as Sadie commanded. They were standing in her newly decorated living room, and she was eager to see how Sadie had made it over. In fact, she desperately needed something to lift her spirits. It was already Wednesday evening, and the cavalry—in the way of an investor—had yet to come to Mac's rescue.

Unless someone showed up with a fat checkbook in the next forty-eight hours, the film wouldn't be finished in time for the upcoming round of festivals, where it could attract a possible distributor, now that Royalton wouldn't be performing that function—or any other—for the film. Even worse, without new money to replace Royalton's investment, the movie might have to be shelved altogether.

But Tally didn't want to think about that just now. The excitement in Sadie's voice was contagious as she shouted, *"Voilà!"*

Tally opened her eyes, and what she saw took her breath away. While the living room had been previously devoid of any color, it was now painted a beautiful sunny yellow that contrasted perfectly with the stark white of its deep moldings. Sheer white drapes hung on high rods, encasing the long, low windows and French doors leading out to the terrace and the pool. A berry-colored patterned kilim rug softened the wide-planked oak floor.

The furniture Sadie had chosen was French country in flavor: lots of whitewashed knotty pine and elegant oval-backed chairs upholstered in a soft blue toile pattern that played well off the red, yellow, and blue stripes on the Louis XV cane-backed Canapé sofa. An intricate crewel tapestry hung on one wall, and a large, square, ornate coffee table showcased two large white stone candlesticks shaped like cherubs. The plain fireplace mantel had been replaced with an ornate one boasting a subtle gargoyle on each side.

Tally's eyes welled up with tears. "I feel like I'm back in Paris. Thank you, Sadie! It's so beautiful."

"Oh, honey, I enjoyed doing it." A tear dotted Sadie's cheek, but she started to laugh as she wiped it away. "Hey, just wait until you see your new screening room! Every movie star needs one, right?"

Tally nodded. "Sadie, I don't know what to say."

"Well, I do know one way you can make it up to me. Would you mind if I invited a few people over to see what I've done?" she asked hopefully. "One of my neighbors in Malibu has been begging me to give her some advice on how she can redo her ballroom before her next gala—"

"Ballroom? Wow! Just how big is her place?"

"Let me put it this way: it makes the Montage BH look like a shed. I'm talking about her Bel Air estate, of course. Her Malibu place is only *half* that size." Sadie chuckled. "Believe me, with the number of parties she throws, she certainly needs a ballroom. Her name is Elena Hahn, and she's a billionairess from Russia. I know you'll recognize her when you see her—she's on every charity's hit list. Her husband is a big oil mogul over in Moscow. In fact, I think her Fabergé egg collection once belonged to the tsar." Sadie shook her head in wonder. "She dabbles in everything, art, antiques, and the other day, she bought a race horse just because it won some charity race she attended at Hollywood Park. The horse hasn't lost since! I tell you, everything that woman touches turns to gold."

She played with one of the window sheers until it

gathered to her liking. "But Elena tells me all those society stiffs bore the heck out of her. I guess that's why
she's a real celebrity hound. She says creative types
are 'wonderful creatures.' Ha! She'd change her mind
after one day in my old job. I guess what Josh does and
the people he does it for fascinate her."

Tally laughed. "Lucky for her you know a lot of creative types."

"Well, you know what they say. Money and power
draw people like bees to honey—even famous people."

Money is power, and both trump fame. It seemed
to Tally that she'd heard that somewhere else before.
Now that she was experiencing it firsthand in her own
career, she had no doubt about how true it was.

Sadie picked up one of the cushions on the couch
and gave it a punch. In response, it puffed back out,
and she nodded to herself, satisfied. "When Elena
heard I was putting together the living room for *the*
Tally Jones, star of her absolute favorite television
show, *Dana Point,* she was pea green with envy. She's
just dying to see how this project turned out."

Tally shrugged. "Sure, bring her over." She started
to walk toward the dining room to see what changes
awaited her there, when a thought suddenly hit her.
"Sadie, why don't you and Josh bring Elena over tomorrow evening, say, around seven? I want to throw
a little dinner party in honor of my new screening

room. In fact, Charles Fourret and Archer Conway, my costars in *Cloistered*, are in town doing some post-dubbing, and I'll see if they're free. Kent Whitman will come, too. Elena should enjoy meeting all of them." Tally raised one of the candlesticks and touched the cheek of the cherub gently with her fingertip. "And of course, she'll want to meet the Oscar-winning producer Mac Carlton. None of *us* will bore her. In fact, we might be her golden ticket into Hollywood."

"That sounds great," Sadie said excitedly. "Let's invite Mandy, too."

"I don't know, Sadie," Tally said, feeling guilty already. "Do you think Elena might be put off by a porn star?"

"Just wait," Sadie said with a short laugh. "You haven't met Elena yet!"

Mac didn't want to bring the rough cut of *Cloistered* to her house, but she reassured him that it would be worth it. "Sadie's new rich friend might be our movie's salvation. By the way, bring Charles and Archer, too. I'm sure they'll appreciate a meal that isn't delivered via room service."

Mac laughed. "Frankly, considering our new austerity plan, I'm sure they'd appreciate anything that didn't come from In-N-Out Burger."

"Great, then we're all set," Tally said. "Just be at my place at seven and ready to make the pitch of your career."

"I guess you're right, we've got nothing to lose. Besides, the clock is ticking."

Since Tally wouldn't be done shooting until at least six, Sadie went ahead and arranged for a meal to be delivered from Spago and ordered enough flower arrangements from Eric Buterbaugh, the premier florist to the stars, to dot every room. She set everything up and made sure the lights were low and inviting. When Tally arrived home, she was relieved to see a full bar ready for her guests as well.

She gave Sadie a kiss. "Wow, you are amazing! You thought of everything."

Guests started trickling in soon after, and Elena Hahn was the last to arrive. What with her tight, low-cut blouse, high boots, and short skirt, the chesty, brassy blonde could have passed for an extra in one of Mandy's movies as opposed to the demure social butterfly Tally had envisioned, but the ten-karat D-class pink diamond ring on her finger certainly put things in perspective. She had a raucously heady laugh, and a deep Slavic accent laced her conversation. "*Yooo* are my favorite actress on TV, Meez Tally Jones! We now will be great friends, *yah*?"

"I look forward to it, Elena. And please do meet my

other guests: the actress Taylor Made and the French director Charles Fourret."

Elena's eyes lit up when the illustrious French director bent down to kiss her hand.

"Charles and Archer Conway are here dubbing the movie we all made together," Tally explained. "In fact, at dinner, you'll be sitting between our director, Kent Whitman, and our producer, Mac Carlton." Mac's handshake was less demonstrative than Charles's but no less heartfelt.

Once all of the introductions had been made and everyone was seated in the dining room, Tally clapped her hands to get her guests' attention. "We have a great treat. After dinner, we'll be moving into my new screening room to view a rough cut of *Cloistered*."

Elena looked at Mac in awe.

Great, thought Tally. *Here's hoping she likes what she sees.*

Even without sound effects or the music dubbed in, the last scene of the movie was chilling, with Tally's character, Emma, running for her life from the man she thought was her savior but who in fact had his hand in the atrocities that had all but destroyed her village.

Out of the corner of her eye, Tally watched as tears

dropped onto Elena's cheeks, and there was silence until Josh rose to flip on a light.

Everyone seemed a bit dazed, then one by one rose to applaud Kent, who in turn clapped ecstatically at Mac.

Mac acknowledged the accolades with a nod of his head. "Thank you all for being a part of this grand adventure. And let's hope this isn't the end of the road."

That roused Elena from her emotional trance. "What do you mean by that, Mac?"

"I got word from Royalton earlier this week that they are pulling their funding from the film. Apparently, they don't see the merit in it."

"How could that be? In my homeland, Belarus, my aunt was persecuted for being a nun. This could have been her story! And you, Tally, you are quite an actress. This film must be seen by millions of people!"

Mac took her hand in his and looked her straight in the eye. "Perhaps you can help us, Elena. You understand this project. Would you agree to replace Royalton as the film's principal backer?"

"I would be honored to finance this movie," Elena said. She seemed genuinely touched to have been asked. "What is the amount you need?"

Mac hesitated a second before saying, "Twenty million."

Tally was on edge as Elena walked slowly out of the

room, toward the front foyer. *Well, there goes our last hope,* she thought.

When Elena reappeared a moment later, she had her Louis Vuitton clutch with her. From it, she pulled a checkbook. "More fun than a race horse, my friends. Now, we should talk percentages and points?"

Hours later, after all the guests had left and the last candle had been extinguished, Mac and Tally went outside to look up at the stars. As they sat together in one of the double chaise longues by the pool, he'd just taught her how to tell a comet from a satellite—how the former shot straight across the horizon, while the other hovered somewhat awkwardly in the sky as it made its way across—when he asked softly, "Will you marry me?"

She turned toward him to see if she could make out his face. "You would marry me, despite the fact that your parents think so little of me?" Her voice trembled as she asked.

"I don't need their approval to love you. I only need yours."

He kissed her, but it wasn't a kiss of desire. It was the kiss of a man who had found his way home.

You're my home, too, Tally thought.

Memories rolled over her: the two of them in Paris,

their small daily rituals at work and at play, the many ways he showed his obvious pride in her. Then, for some reason, she remembered the bearded stranger who had hovered around her during her waitressing stint at the Sunset Tower on the night of *Vanity Fair*'s Oscar party.

Tally bolted upright. "Oh my God! That was you!"

"What was me? What are you talking about?"

"The burger monster! The guy who kept coming up to me for more cheeseburgers that night at the Sunset Tower!"

Mac laughed so hard he almost fell off the chaise. "You just figured that out *now*?"

"Well, you have to admit, you did look different with that crazy beard."

All of a sudden, his face went serious. "I was a fool that night. I saw Gabriel make his move, and my ego was bruised, so I walked away instead of introducing myself to the most gorgeous woman I'd ever seen."

"Oh." Tally leaned back into his arms. "I guess in life, timing really is everything."

"You can say that again. I could have talked to you at Sadie and Josh's wedding, too, but by the time I got up the nerve, again Gabriel had found you first. You were standing on that terrace overlooking the ocean. Do you remember?"

"You were there, too? Wow." Tally took a moment

to let that sink in. Finally, she said, "Mac Carlton, I love you with all my heart. And you've proven you love me. You've waited for me. You've bet your career on me. What other man would do that? I would love to marry you."

She sealed her words with a kiss. Then they made love, right there, under the stars.

Chapter 25

THE ANNOUNCEMENT OF their engagement ran as a one-liner in the Hitched column of *Variety*, in its usual understated style—"Tally Jones and Mac Carlton, on November 15 in Bel Air, Calif. Jones is an actress, Carlton is an independent film producer"—but that didn't keep it from being big news in Hollywood. In no time at all, their engagement was being touted in *People*, Page Six, and *Us Weekly*.

"I like the idea of a big wedding," Mac said to Tally over breakfast that Sunday. "You're a big star, so why not?"

"I guess it's because I'm in the limelight so much anyway that something this personal seems like it should be just us—along with friends and family, of course."

The minute the words were out, she wished she hadn't said them. Mac's face clouded over at the thought of how his parents had rejected her. She then realized that by having a big wedding, he felt she might forget how cruel they were to her. To *him*.

She could do that for him. For both of them.

Tally put on a big smile and threw her arms around his neck. "You know what? We might as well invite everyone we know and make it the party of a lifetime. Why not?"

Over drinks at the Polo Lounge later that afternoon, Tally asked Mandy and Sadie if they would be her bridesmaids. When they were through squealing, she turned serious. "Sadie, I'd like to ask you another favor. Are you up to the challenge of planning another wedding? We're going into sweeps season, and things are so hectic on the show—"

Sadie nearly spit out her martini. "Of course!" Taking a moment to consider, she added, "But if you want to give Mac Hollywood's 'wedding of the decade,' I suggest we call in the big guns. You know, someone who really knows about planning an epic event."

Tally sighed but nodded. "OK, sure. And who would that be?"

"Preston Bailey, of course! He did the Donald's wedding and Liza Minnelli's and Melissa River's, too. In fact, Preston will be Josh's and my gift to you. I'll run interference, of course."

Tally laughed. "Do you think Josh could throw Mac's bachelor party? Or am I asking for trouble, considering how things turned out at his own?"

Sadie frowned. "I still haven't let him off the hook for Susie's little gift. With all the long hours he's been working lately, I'm beginning to wonder if the party she threw him wasn't just a one-time thing."

"Long hours are part of the job," Tally reassured her. "You saw it when you worked there, too."

"Yeah, sure, I saw a *lot* of things. And that's what scares me." Sadie took a long, slow sip of her drink. "Oh, maybe I'm just overreacting. It's just that I feel as if I've been replaced in his life. It doesn't help that all my calls go through Seth. I'm used to picking up the phone and talking to Josh twenty times a day."

"But now that you're not his assistant, wouldn't that be an awful lot?" Tally asked.

Sadie laughed. "Yeah, I guess you're right. I just know how easy it would be for Josh to fall back into some of his old bad habits." She sat up straight. "I'll tell you what, if he behaves himself during Mac's bachelor party, I'll know I'm just imagining things."

"Hey, speaking of parties, I'm going to take on the

task of throwing you a bachelorette party *par excellence*," Mandy announced.

Tally and Sadie exchanged concerned glances. Tally started to say something, but Mandy held up a finger to silence her.

"Before you say anything, I'm laying down a rule of my own: no matter how much you beg, *no strippers*."

Tally showed her appreciation with a deep sigh of relief.

"Unless you absolutely insist on it," she added mischievously. "Then, of course, I'll work my contacts and pull together one hot show. *Just kidding!* What do you take me for, some kind of skank? I'm thinking a high tea at the Hotel Bel-Air. Hats and gloves mandatory. G-strings optional."

"I can't believe she actually hooked him! *Ooooh,* that just makes my blood *boil*." Susie threw her copy of *People* on the floor and pushed her eye mask back over her lids. Jared, her neurotic costar, had been keeping her up late at night, and she was particularly cranky this morning. No matter how many times she'd warned herself that screwing a costar only led to hurt feelings when the inevitable happened—her stomping on his heart, just for kicks—she just couldn't help herself when it came to buff young buns with stiff cocks.

And Jared could sure keep it up.

Making and keeping him angry helped keep things hot in the bedroom, and every chance she got, she played on his easy tendency toward jealousy. Lately, she'd been flirting with Spencer Cowle, the actor who played her husband, Hank, on *Dana Point*. Already, Jared had threatened Spencer one night when he ran into him in the men's room of Dan Tana's. Poor Spencer couldn't just come out and tell Jared that he was in the closet, which made the whole incident even funnier when Jared relayed it to Susie. As always, the fight led to some great sex. If you called anal plugs and nipple clips great sex. And Susie did—as long as she was the one doing the plugging and the clipping.

Garfield quit fussing with the wig he was teasing for her and glanced at the magazine, which lay open to the article on Tally and Mac. They looked adorable in the photo, which had been taken by some pap while they walked hand-in-hand through the Farmer's Market. He gave a grudging nod. "Well, if it's any consolation, you're not the only one. Miss Elizabeth isn't too happy about it, either."

Susie yanked the mask off one eye. "Who the hell is Miss Elizabeth? What are you babbling about?"

Garfield's back stiffened with pride. "I was referring to the legendary actress Elizabeth Hayden Carlton. She happens to be Richard Carlton's wife—which also makes her the darling groom's mama. Many of us from the studio's glory days still remember her as a sweet young thing, and no one but *moi* has touched a thinning hair on her precious head since her contract days."

Susie sniffed. "And why does *she* rate?"

"Darling, it's one of the perks of being married to the boss man."

Susie's lips curled up on one side. "Ha. Must be nice. Get back to what you were saying about her being pissed at Mac."

Garfield didn't need much prompting. "Well, if you must know, she is just fit to be tied about his pending nuptials. She actually called Tally Jones a slut—and a druggie—to her face! Heaven knows where her poor addled little brain came up with *that*."

Susie batted her lashes innocently. "Truth be told, that one's been floating around for quite some time. And you know what they say: where's there's smoke, there's fire."

Garfield gave her a knowing glance. "I can just imagine who lit the match on *that* one."

Susie shrugged. "So, when is Miss Elizabeth due back for her next appointment?"

"Tomorrow, as a matter of fact, right at five. When it comes to her hair color, she prefers ebony to ivory. I do her color, then Sir Richard takes her home in the corporate limo."

"My last scene shoots at three. Maybe I'll pay you a little visit afterward. You know, to keep the old girl company. I'm guessing she'll like that."

Susie assigned the task of finding Gabriel McNamara to Jared, and he came through with flying colors. Through their mutual pot dealer, he'd tracked Gabriel down at the Venice Beach cottage of one of his old buddies, where he'd been crashing on the couch ever since being terminated from his job on *Intensive Care* and blacklisted by every studio in town.

He gladly accepted Susie's invitation to meet her for a drink at the Viceroy and, after four Stoli martinis, Susie's overt display of cleavage, and some gentle prodding, he told her about defiling Tally Jones.

"Honey, eh?" Just the thought of it had Susie licking her lips. "Yummy. Sounds like fun."

"Yeah. I guess it's a fetish of mine." He stared at her breasts as he said this, and she knew just what he was thinking.

Some honey-coated tit for tat would certainly be in order, if and when he completed the mission she was about to assign him. To make him more amenable, she slowly undid another button on her sheer blouse so that even more of her black lace bra was exposed. "Oh, I'm sure she loved every minute of it. But I'll just bet she squealed about it to that boyfriend she was two-timing you with—you know, that producer Mac Carlton—so that he'd be jealous. In fact, I'm guessing he made up some kind of story about you raping her and went crying to his daddy. That's probably why you got canned, Gabriel. And what a shame, too." She clicked her tongue in mock despair. "Word gets around fast in this town. No one wants to hire a rapist."

"But I'm not a rapist! I tell you, she wanted it!" His hand shook violently as he lifted his martini glass to his lips and downed what was left in it. "Damn bastard!"

"He's marrying her, too."

Gabriel's anger deflated. "Yeah, I heard. It's all over the press."

"I find the best revenge is always ruining an engagement, and I've got an idea. It'll take a bit of acting, but you can fake an illness, right? Of course you can! You were Dr. Sam Jeffries. You cured them all."

He leaned in closer. It was easy to listen to Susie's scheme while he imagined pouring honey on those big, sweet breasts.

Chapter 26

TALLY HAD FORGOTTEN that she'd scheduled her doctor's appointment for just three days before the wedding. She made up her mind to go anyway. It was just supposed to be an annual checkup, so she'd be out of there in half an hour, tops.

But after her exam, Tally's gynecologist started asking some odd questions. Had she been feeling more tired lately? Yes, answered Tally, but between working so hard on the show and planning a wedding, that was to be expected, right? As for the question about when she last had her period, Tally had to pause for a moment. "Hmmm." That was a stumper, but it shouldn't have been. Maybe . . . no . . . certainly before . . .

"Gee," Tally finally said weakly, "I guess it was longer ago than I thought." Then the implication hit her. "Oh my God! Should I pee on a stick?"

The doctor smiled. "Your urine sample is what tipped me off. Tally, you're pregnant."

She knew it couldn't be Gabriel's. The timing wasn't right. To make sure, Tally did the math backward and had the doctor double-check it. From what they could tell, it had happened at least several weeks after she'd returned from Paris.

Mac and I are going to have a baby, she thought. She wanted to laugh and cry all at the same time. She floated out of the doctor's office on a cloud.

Her first instinct was to pick up the phone and call Mac, but then she thought better of it. She'd much rather give him the news on the night of their honeymoon. She wouldn't even tell Sadie or Mandy—he'd have to hear it first.

She got back to the set just in time to get made up for her next scene. But when Ben asked her why she had a "big naughty grin" on her face, all she could do was giggle uncontrollably. He presumed it was honeymoon anticipation and laughed along with her.

Tally's last scene of the day finished at seven. Exhausted, she went back to her trailer to change and clean up. The scene had been just between her and

Jared, who, now that he was hanging with Susie, was acting like a paranoid pain in the ass. Between takes, he'd gone so far as to accuse her of sabotaging his career, whatever that meant. Instead of waiting to find out, she'd asked Burt to assign her a security guard. She wasn't taking any chances now that she was carrying a baby. He groused at first but gave in. He didn't like Jared, either, since he'd fallen under Susie's spell.

Needless to say, when Tally answered the knock on her trailer door, the last person she expected to see standing there was Gabriel McNamara.

"What the hell are you doing here?" She looked around for her security detail, but he was nowhere in sight.

"Calm down, Tally. I'm not going to hurt you. I was never going to hurt you." Gabriel looked and sounded like a broken man. "I had an audition on the lot," he continued. "My first since I got kicked off my show."

"Oh. Well . . . how did it go?" Tally clutched the neck of her robe tightly. She was going to stall as long as she had to, until her security guy showed up.

"OK. It's not much of a role, but it's for a feature film." His eyes glassed up. "I'm beginning to think that no one will hire me ever again."

That got to Tally, and she sighed deeply. The last time she saw Gabriel was not the way she wanted to remember him.

"Look, Tally, can I come in for a minute? I just . . . well, I want to apologize. But I don't want to do it out here."

She thought about it for a few long, hard moments, then stepped aside so he could follow her in.

As he crossed the threshold, he gave her a hug, squeezing her tightly. There was such desperation in it that it stunned her, and she froze. The next thing she knew, his lips were all over her. She didn't have time to react, and they stumbled into the trailer as he closed the door behind her.

Finally, she was able to shove him off. "I'm calling security now!" she said, and ran to the door.

"No! Please." He gasped. "You don't understand. I've taken too many pills for my anxiety disorder, and I'm a little out of it. I'm dizzy as hell. Look, just let me sit here for a bit. If anyone sees me like this, I'll never get the part. Can you just get me some water? That would help a lot." Not sure what to do, Tally went into the bathroom. At least there was a lock on that door, so if he tried any funny business, she'd just shut herself in.

When she came out with a glass of water, he was already gone. He'd left a note that read, *Sorry, babe. Forgive me.*

So that was his apology.

Rattled, she walked to her car and drove home. On

the way, she decided not to say anything to Mac about the incident. He'd be upset, and the last thing she needed was for him to worry about her right before the wedding.

She'd prefer that he save his worry for afterward—when he found out she was carrying their child.

"It's very kind of you to meet with me, Mr. Carlton—Mac. You don't mind if I call you by your first name, do you?" Susie looked innocently across the table at her dinner guest.

Although it was just two nights before their wedding, Mac had gone ahead and agreed to take a meeting with the actress Susie Sheppard. Since Burt Tillman, that cheap son of a bitch, wouldn't let Tally off for even a day or two before her own wedding and the episode she was shooting wouldn't wrap until probably midnight, he figured he might as well work, too. Besides, the project Susie had pitched him over the phone sounded intriguing, something about a three-way love triangle and a double-cross.

He'd never met Susie, but he had heard a lot about her. Not all of it good, granted. But you could never believe what you read in the newspapers. He and Tally were proof of that. And while he knew Tally didn't care much for her, Susie was too well connected to write off totally.

She had insisted that they meet at the Hotel Bel Air, where she had taken a villa suite. "My home is being renovated, so these are temporary digs," she explained. They ate in the suite's living room, and between bites of their main course and sips of wine, she chattered away. As she went on about work, Susie told him that she felt as if she already knew him, since Tally talked about him all the time on the set of *Dana Point*.

When she mentioned Tally, her bright smile turned into a frown. "Unfortunately, I wish I could tell you what she says is flattering, but I don't want to start our friendship with a lie, Mac. You see, it's so shameful, the way she's using you. I can't in good conscience attend the wedding, knowing what she's divulged to me."

She went on to say that Tally was telling everyone she'd pulled the wool over his eyes and that because he was so smitten with her, her career would always be taken care of. "You know, Mac, it wouldn't be so sad if—well, if she wasn't two-timing you."

Mac couldn't believe his ears. "You're lying," he growled, then stood up. "Check please," he said to the waiter.

"Hey, if you don't believe me, you can see with your

own two eyes." Susie pulled out her iPhone. There, in a video clip dated just the night before, Gabriel stood outside Tally's dressing room. Tally was dressed in a bathrobe, and she and Gabriel hugged and kissed before she pulled him inside her dressing room with him.

Susie paused the video. "Gabriel McNamara is her old boyfriend, isn't he?"

He nodded, stunned.

"A security camera picked this up. I caught a couple of the security guys laughing about it, and I couldn't have them doing that to poor Tally or to poor *you!*" She batted her eyes at him sympathetically. "So I paid them to give me this clip from the computer, and I made sure they erased the rest. Unfortunately, it gets worse."

Susie started the video again. In what looked like the inside of Tally's dressing room, a naked Tally could be seen on top of Gabriel, her back to the camera as they made love.

Mac was dumbfounded. *So, I guess my father was right about Tally after all.*

As he stared off into space, Susie poured him a stiff drink. Before he knew it, she was also rubbing his shoulders. He put the glass to his lips and downed it in one gulp. She refilled it quickly.

"Look, Mac, I'm sorry you had to find out this way.

It really breaks my heart." Her chest heaved as a crocodile tear rolled down her cheek.

He was touched that this stranger had taken the time to set him straight. And he could tell she was pained to have been the one to break the news to him. Without thinking, he reached over and wiped the tear from her face, and the next thing he knew, she was in his arms, and he was kissing her.

She began undressing him. At first, he was put off by it; he didn't need sympathy sex. But revenge sex . . . well now, that was different.

He didn't make a move as she unzipped his pants. Or when she fondled his cock, expertly, before she leaned him back on the bed and climbed on top of him.

He didn't go home that night. Or the next one, either.

Chapter 27

THE INVITATIONS TO Tally and Mac's wedding had gone out weeks ago. Each came in a large box holding fake stemmed gardenias, and inside was another box holding the invitation, which was embossed with Swarovski crystals and engraved with silver calligraphy.

The wedding was being held at the Beverly Wilshire, where big white vases overflowed with gardenias and orchids that had been picked just the day before. The event had drawn a packed house: three hundred fifty guests, to be exact. RSVPs had come in from all the usual suspects: those who had worked with both Tally and Mac, those who hoped to work with them in the future, friends, and family. Tally's mother and father were there. They'd flown in just that morning, and the pride in their eyes had made her eyes well up with tears. She couldn't wait for them to meet Mac.

If only he'd show up.

Tally's dress—a fifty-thousand-dollar ivory strapless gown, embroidered with Chantilly lace, with a drop-waist bodice and silk organza ruffle on an A-line skirt—had been a gift from Monique Lhuillier, and Tally looked like a princess. But where was her prince?

The morning after her late night of shooting, Tally had called Sadie, frantic. "Mac never came home last night. Did he go out with Josh? Did they do the bachelor-party thing after all?"

Tally's question had thrown Sadie for a loop. Although Josh had offered to host one, Mac passed on the suggestion. "Heck, no. Josh got home late, but that's nothing new. And he certainly didn't act as if he'd been out having a good time."

"OK." Tally tried to keep the worry out of her voice. "I'm sure he slept at the studio. They've been working pretty late nights, trying to get the film completed. And with us leaving for a weeklong honeymoon, I'm sure he wanted to finish up a lot of things."

But it turned out he wasn't at the studio. His assistant, Carole, said he'd mentioned a dinner meeting for a possible new project the night before and had called in earlier and said he wasn't going to be in all day.

Well, OK, Tally thought, *he deserves to take a day for himself. Especially the day before his wedding. But why wouldn't he call and let me know, too?*

To keep her mind off Mac, she had met Sadie and Preston at the Wilshire to take in the drama of the setup. Even through the hustle and bustle, though, she couldn't help but think something was wrong, or he would have called.

By eight o'clock that night, he still hadn't shown up or even checked in. At least, he hadn't checked in with *her.* Carole had gotten a text message that read, *Since I'll be on my honeymoon next week, feel free to check messages from your place. Have a nice week!—Mac.*

Hearing that left Tally a bit relieved, until midnight rolled around and Mac still hadn't shown up, let alone returned her increasingly frantic voice messages.

And now here she was, waiting in the hotel's penthouse suite for word of him on the day of their wedding, while many floors below her, a ballroom filled with people wondered when Mac would appear and turn toward the center aisle in anticipation of his captivatingly beautiful bride.

The look on Sadie's face as she entered the penthouse suite was a mix of shock, concern, and pity. She didn't have to say a word. Tally already knew Mac wasn't coming. He had stood her up, and he hadn't even had the guts to call and tell her why.

As she blacked out, she heard Sadie yell to Mandy to call for a doctor.

Later that evening, when she'd finally made it home, there was a small, unmarked package waiting for her on the doorstep. *It has to be from him,* she thought.

Her hands shook as she opened it. There was no note, just a DVD: Anxiously, she put it in her DVD player and let it roll. The video was grainy but clear enough for her to make out the two people in it: Susie and Mac.

She couldn't believe her eyes, but no there was no mistaking the two of them. Tally winced as she saw the way Susie led Mac into one passionate act after another. Their foreplay was vicious, and when Susie took him in her mouth, he grimaced. There was no pleasure in his groan.

Not that it mattered. *He's there with Susie, not here with me.*

As Mac finally mounted Susie, Tally heard her cry out, "But what about Tally?"

Mac paused for just a moment before growling, "Fuck Tally."

As he drove deep inside her, Susie gasped. "Whatever you say."

Tally stared at the video in freeze-frame for what felt like hours. Then she went upstairs to her bedroom to cry.

"Has she heard?" Mandy stared across the kitchen island at Sadie. In her hand were all of the weekly celebrity magazines.

"Of course she's heard. It's all over the television and the Web." Angrily, Sadie tossed the magazines toward the trash can but missed. The headline on *People* stared up at her: "Altared States: Susie's In, Tally's Out!" The photo showed a supremely happy Susie Sheppard, wearing the exact gown that had been designed for Tally, on the arm of her groom, Mac Carlton.

On the floor, *OK! Magazine* was opened to the spread of the story, informing readers about "the posh affair at the renowed Beverly Wilshire Hotel—which happened only a day after Carlton was supposed to have married Tally Jones in the same place. Afterward, the groom, along with his surprise bride, retired to the hotel's penthouse suite."

"That bitch! She not only stole the love of Tally's life, she stole her wedding, too!" Mandy gave the magazine a kick with the pointy toe of her Jimmy Choo and sent it fluttering into the air.

"I guess Mac got exactly what he wanted." Both girls turned to see Tally standing in the doorway. Her eyes were sunken into her puffy red lids.

Mandy ran to Tally and threw her arms around her. "He's a complete idiot."

Tally smiled sadly as she shook her head. "No. It's Susie, up to her old tricks. She made up some lie about me and got to Mac. I'm sure of it."

Mandy grimaced. "Well, whatever it was, it must have been a beauty. But what I don't get is why he didn't at least talk to you about it. He could have called *any* of us. We would have set him straight."

Tally shook her head again. "No, he would have presumed you were covering for me. That's why he's avoiding you, too."

Suddenly, guilt clouded Sadie's face. "Well, he has called Josh. Mac is contracting Susie for his next movie."

Tally sat down hard on one of the kitchen stools. "She's going to be starring in his next film?"

"I'm sorry you had to hear it from me, Tally." Sadie looked tortured. "But I might as well tell you the clincher. Josh is insisting we have the two of them over for dinner. He says they're Hollywood's new 'power couple.' Can you believe that? Of course, I told him where he could shove that idea, but he didn't like it. Apparently, Susie wants to smooth things over between us—"

"You should do it." Tally had never sounded more resolute.

Sadie's eyes were dead. Make that *deadly*. "Hell, no! Not in a million years."

"I mean it, Sadie. Play nice. Kiss ass. What happened between Mac and me is old news." She reached down, grabbed the magazines, and crammed them into the trash can. "I don't want 'jilted celebrity' to be my identity, and I'm going to make sure that label doesn't stick." She ran her hand through her hair, which hadn't been combed in days. "In fact, I've got to get back to work. *Today.*"

"But . . ." Mandy bit back the words as she and Sadie exchanged concerned glances.

Tally turned to her friend. "But what?"

"Just . . . Susie will be there."

Tally held her head high and straightened her shoulders. This was the worst night. *When am I going to wake up?* she thought. "That's OK. I'm sure she'd like me off the set as badly as I want to leave. If she doesn't have Josh working on that already, then I will soon enough."

Sadie and Mandy didn't know Tally was pregnant, but they knew their friend well enough to know she still loved Mac. What she didn't tell them and what she was almost too afraid to admit to herself was that in her heart, she held out hope that he'd come back to her.

Unlike Tally, Susie relished the opportunity to act with her nemesis. In fact, she lived for their scenes together. She loved being in her face.

To fuel the already white-hot fire, she'd ordered a production assistant to hold her cell phone just off camera and to call out to her between takes that Mac was dying to talk to her, right then and there. To drive the point home, when she grabbed the phone, she'd pretend they were talking dirty.

Tally pretended to ignore her, but Susie knew she heard every word.

Susie had also worked over Burt to put them in as many scenes together as possible. Of course, he had agreed. He was no fool; he knew what a ratings bonanza he had on his hands.

It was obvious that Tally was miserable, but she was stuck. She had another four years to go on her contract. The only thing she could do in her situation to make it more bearable was to act rings around Susie, which she did. This only made Susie angrier, especially since Susie was now being written as the long-suffering heroine, and Tally was being written up as the bad girl, yet the viewers still sided with Tally. If they didn't outright say it in their fan mail, they made it known that they loved to hate her.

"I can't believe it! *I'm* the one they should love," she told Burt, pouting.

He just laughed in her face—and all the way to the bank.

Tally felt the queasiness first, then the cramping, but she ignored both.

Then came the blood. Lots of it. Her costar, Spencer Cowle, actually caught her when she passed out for a moment.

Larry, the director, insisted she go lie down in her trailer. Instead, she drove herself to her doctor's office. The doctor put her on the stirrups and searched for a fetal heartbeat, but there was none. "You're miscarrying," she said gravely. "We have to perform a D and C. We can do it here. For your privacy." Tally cried as they put her under.

When she woke up, she cried even harder. She'd lost the one thing that would have made her happy, that could have allowed her to hold on to a piece of Mac forever. She'd lost their child.

It's for the best, she told herself. But she knew better.

Three Years Later

Chapter 28

*B*REATHE IN, Tally commanded herself. *Breathe out. Now smile.*

She was at the Oscars and once again a nominee. This time, she was up for Best Supporting Actress in a Motion Picture for her performance in a Paul Haggis ensemble piece, *Shattered*, that had gotten great buzz throughout the awards season.

Her first nomination had been for Best Actress for *Cloistered*. She'd won, and the movie won, too, for Best Picture. For Tally, it had been a hollow victory. In his acceptance speech, Mac had singled out various members of the cast and crew, including the film's angel producer, Elena Hahn, but he'd never uttered Tally's name. Was it an oversight, she had wondered, or in deference to his new bride, Susie Sheppard Carlton? Tally still winced every time she heard that name spoken out loud.

In Tally's speech, given just a few minutes before, she had thanked Mac for the honor of working with him and for recognizing a newcomer's talent. When the cameras cut to him in the audience, he was caught in a stone-faced stare. Despite his cold response, she felt any debt she might have owed him was now paid in full.

Since *Cloistered*, Tally had chosen her film projects carefully, seeking out roles that challenged her. This had paid off wonderfully, with two Golden Globe nods and two more Oscar nominations for her film work. Perhaps tonight she would add another win to her résumé.

As for her work on *Dana Point*, Golden Globe, WGA, and Emmy awards kept coming as well. Year after year, she'd become the one to beat in the category of Outstanding Actress in a Drama Series.

As her limousine slowed down in front of the Kodak Theater's red carpet, Tally tapped the window that separated her from John, her driver, initiating their long-held prearranged cue that the limo's slow crawl could now come to a complete stop.

Two hulking security goons approached the limo and opened her door. Their presence was supposed to provide additional reassurance that the cheering mob was safely contained on the other side of the clear plastic-fronted bleachers. It never ceased to amaze her that a piece of plastic, let alone a flimsy piece of red velvet rope, could so successfully serve as a psychological barrier to those who aspired to rub elbows with the A-list. And Tally had never forgotten what it was like to be on the other side of those partitions.

By the time she emerged from her limo chrysalis, she had shaken off her innate shyness and morphed into a full-fledged diva, pausing for a few moments in order to wave graciously to the crowd that shouted out her name.

With her patented Tally Jones smile plastered on her lips, she gave the paparazzi her practiced pose (half-turned torso, head tilted down and to the left, chest thrust up and out, and dead-on gaze—all part of the drill), never once letting on that she'd been temporarily blinded by the halo of light emanating from the cameras that snapped around her.

Finally, a headset-wearing flack in black took her gently by the elbow and escorted her through a sea of overly coiffed (albeit studiously disheveled), signature-scented, air-kissing humanity, all primed to the nines in their gowns and tuxes, so that she could share a few moments of radiance with the various red-carpet reporters from *E!*, *Entertainment Tonight*, *Extra*, and

Access Hollywood, just to name a few. Without fail, all of the talking heads asked her how she felt about her nomination (very excited; it never gets old; it's always an honor) and whom she was wearing (her pale blue body-hugging gown was Atelier Versace; the three-inch Swarovski diamond-encrusted stilettos were YSL, the diamonds dripping from her ears, neck, and wrists were all Neil Lane), in between paying her effusive compliments on both her performance and her dress.

Right as she was about to make some clever comment to Ryan Seacrest, just over his shoulder, she spotted Susie, who had her arm clasped on Mac's like a shackle. That would have been OK, except that just at that moment, Mac glanced over at Tally, too.

The way he looked at her—with utter contempt—made her falter. Ryan covered nicely for her, and when the camera cut away, they both had a good laugh. Of course, he didn't know she had only laughed to keep from crying.

Tally didn't win that night, but she wasn't disappointed. She had once believed that the biggest thing that could happen to her would be to win an Oscar, and now that she had one on her mantel, she knew that wasn't true.

Susie had no Oscar, but as far as Tally was concerned, she had won the biggest prize of all. She had Mac.

〰

Ever since he had left Tally, Mac hated attending the annual *Vanity Fair* party. He had to go in order to see and be seen, but every second hurt. It reminded him too much of the first time he saw her.

Tonight at the party, Tally seemed to be everywhere. He glanced up at one point to see Scorsese deep in conversation with her. Twenty minutes later, Tarantino was pitching her one of his Tarantino-esque plots. An hour went by, and there she was, sharing some inside joke with Halle and Hilary. When Clooney cornered her, Mac's heart fell through a pit in his stomach.

Susie, who he knew had only been pretending to listen to Elizabeth complain about once again being overlooked for the Kennedy Center Honors, nudged Mac sharply. "What are you staring at?"

Of course, she knew. To make a point, she pressed her lips into his. *Hard.*

He knew she hoped Tally was watching, and he resented the hell out of her for it. They'd been married for three years now, and he still didn't know what to make of his wife. His anger over how Tally had used him, coupled with the intoxicating sex with Susie, had spurred Mac to do the most impulsive thing he'd ever done in his life: ask a woman he'd known for less than forty-eight hours to marry him. Just as impulsively (at least, it had seemed that way), Susie had said yes to his offer, and there was no turning back from there.

He'd thought it somewhat odd how enthusiastic both of his parents had been at the news that he'd dumped Tally for Susie. Richard had called her "an outstanding young woman," while Elizabeth had raved about how sweet she was. (By sheer coincidence, she'd met Susie the week before, through the hairdresser the two women shared.)

It had also surprised him how quickly Susie had pulled together the wedding—not to mention how she had insisted on holding it at the same place he was to have married Tally. But Susie's reason for doing so seemed perfectly logical at the time, and somewhat romantic: she claimed she'd dreamed of having a wedding there since she was a little girl. Afterward, when his assistant, Carole, had shown him an article that detailed, point by point, all the ways in which Susie had copied Tally's wedding plans, he knew he should ask her about it. In fact, he started to bring it up once, but he lost his train of thought when she began to unzip him. One thing led to another, and by the time she was through with him, he'd made up his mind that it all had been a big coincidence.

Still, something about her bugged him. He could

never get over the feeling that everything she did or said came with an agenda.

He was a loyal husband, but in truth, he didn't love her. And, the sex sucked. It was like making love to a lobster.

The news that Mandy was pregnant and would soon be getting married took her two closest friends by surprise.

After taking only a second to recover from the shock, Tally gave her a big hug. "That's wonderful, Mandy," she said. "Who's the lucky daddy?"

"None of the usual suspects, if that's what you're thinking. I could never marry someone in the business. Talk about bringing your work home with you. Ewww!" Mandy wrinkled her nose, then got serious. "Actually, it's Collin, my accountant."

Sadie laughed. "You mean that quiet little guy you brought to our Fourth of July party?"

"One and the same. And listen, sorry about him not being more chatty that night. He's just a bit shy."

"That's OK, he gave us a tax tip that saved us a fortune. In fact, Josh is proposing to his partners that they consider him for the agency's business."

Mandy smiled with pride. "That would be awesome!"

"You won't show for a while," Tally said. "When you do, what will that do to your career?"

"Porn stars have babies, too, silly. I've already given notice that I'll be taking a leave of absence, starting immediately. And when I'm back in the saddle, so to speak, we're taking the Taylor Made brand in a whole different direction. Collin and I are going to produce and distribute my films ourselves, and I'm already lining up a stable of actors to brand."

"You've done well with Jerry," Sadie said. "Why would you leave him now?"

"Well, for one thing, my site gets more than five million unique visitors a month. If I can sell direct, I get to cut out the middle man."

"That makes sense," Tally said.

"Besides, I'm bored with acting. I enjoy scripting and directing much more." Tally and Sadie nodded. "Anyway, enough about business. The wedding will be held in Vegas at the Bellagio. For my bridesmaids, I'm thinking hot pink and short, short minidresses."

Tally laughed. "Sounds like a plan. And I believe it's my turn to throw the wedding shower."

Mandy gave her a naughty smile. "No need to worry about offending any of my guests, because most of them will be porn stars—and they expect a great show."

Chapter 29

THE THOUGHT THAT her husband might still be in love with his ex was eating Susie up inside. Of course he was, but Mac would never admit it to her if it were true. But if not for her suspicions, she would have left Mac long ago.

He had begun to bore her before their first anniversary. The sex was decent—at least, it had been in the beginning, when he was still raging over Tally's supposed deceit—but after his anger had subsided, having sex became nonexistent. But she'd already plotted out an exit strategy, and so far, it was going brilliantly.

As an independent producer, Mac could only do so much for her career. But were she to marry a studio head, she'd have the pick of any project on the lot. Therefore, Richard Carlton had become her secret lover.

It hadn't taken much to get Richard's attention, just being in the right place at the right time—specifically, on the lot, after hours. And what the old man lacked in stamina he made up for in staying power, thanks to her stash of baby-blue pills.

Despite juggling two Carltons, she hadn't dropped Jared completely. She'd just relegated him to between-scenes quickies or on the nights Mac worked late and she wasn't seeing Richard. Or Gabriel, who had been right about the delights of honey and the thrill of restraints.

Susie never felt the slightest bit guilty about her behavior. Nor did she wonder if Richard felt guilty about their trysts. He was a studio head, for God's sake. As for making an ass out of his son, she figured that's how he got his rocks off in the first place. *Talk about a dysfunctional family.*

She felt her role of daughter-in-law-with-benefits gave her the right to do whatever the hell she wanted, to whomever she wanted. And that was especially true when it came to Tally.

That morning, when she found out that the script called for Katherine to beg for Jamie's forgiveness during an elegant cocktail party, Susie's gut reaction was *Um, no way in hell.* So when it was time for her to say her line in front of the cameras, she took her very real Cosmopolitan martini and tossed it onto Tally's sparkly silver Hervé Léger bandage dress.

"Just improvising," she murmured to the shocked Tally.

Susie was being a real bitch on set that day, and Tally was in no mood to tolerate it. After taking a second to recover from having a drink thrown at her, she remembered that she knew how to improvise, too. She took a tray of pastries out of a waiter-extra's hand and smacked Susie on the ass with it, leaving her rival's Oscar de la Renta duchess satin, draped one-shoulder dress covered in cream and chocolate.

"Keep rolling! Keep rolling!" Larry Hornsby, the director, hissed to the stunned cameramen.

Tally, shaken but satisfied, turned to leave, but Susie tripped her. Tally almost fell, but she recovered nicely, and in the same movement, she punched Susie in the gut.

As Susie doubled over, Tally smiled triumphantly. Presuming that Susie had had enough, she walked up the grand staircase, only to hear Susie huffing up the steps after her.

No. No more, Tally thought. *This is going to end,*

once and for all. As she paused on the stairs, it all came flooding back to her: the way Susie had humiliated Sadie with that atrocious bridal shower, Susie's ongoing sabotage of her on the set, the demands she made to the producer in order to keep Tally's role from growing on the show, how she had planted lies about Tally in the gossip columns, and worst of all, how Susie had lied to Mac and stolen him away and how the stress of losing Mac had caused Tally to lose their baby.

All of the memories boiled into a rage that Tally could no longer control, and Susie never saw the roundhouse punch coming.

And it was all caught on camera.

Satisfied, Tally walked off the set.

"Fire the bitch this very minute!"

Susie's screeches were giving Burt a headache on top of his already brutal hangover. It was way too early for him to be on the set, but two of the network suits were already there, so of course, he came running, too.

"Shut your pie hole. Tally's lawyers have already been in touch with me. Based on your attack, she feels her safety has been compromised, and her contract has been breached. She's demanded to be released from it, and we're honoring that so that we don't get sued. But she has graciously given us her permission to use the scene, and she said she's available for one more that writes her off."

"*What*? You're *using* it?"

"Hell, yeah! That will go down as the best catfight in the history of television."

"The hell you are! She sucker-punched me—"

"I saw the dailies, Susie. You started the damn fight. If anyone should get fired, it's you." He looked her right in the eye. "Frankly, I think she did you a favor. You might actually get your Emmy this time."

Susie paused to consider that possibility. Unlike Tally's, her movie career was DOA, even with Mac calling in favors left and right. OK, sure, she didn't mind if the scene stayed in. In fact, she'd tell everyone she had suggested it and then done some on-set improv with Tally to make it perfect.

For now, anyway, payback would have to wait.

Chapter 30

NOW THAT SHE was no longer on *Dana Point*, Tally felt completely liberated. She was free to pick from any of the wonderful scripts that arrived for her at Josh's offices from producers and directors requesting that she consider them.

Where do I begin? Tally wondered. There were enough scripts to fill one of her bedrooms, where she arranged them in five rows that were stacked chest-high from the floor.

She placed an armload of scripts on the guest bed. Two of them were old enough that they were already in production with other actresses. With a touch of bitterness, she tossed those onto a pile destined for the recycling bin. While *Dana Point* had given her a lot to be thankful for, this last year in particular, the show had stood in the way of some great movie roles.

She shook off her disappointment. *I have nothing to regret. All I can do is move forward, both in my career and in my personal life.*

By late that afternoon, she had identified three scripts that intrigued her and whose producers were still looking for a lead actress. The project Scorsese had mentioned to her was one. Then there was a Spielberg epic, which looked like fun and had threequel written all over it.

And then there was Mac's latest project, *Tapestry*. It was a period piece filled with intrigue and plot twists, and in the hands of the right actress, it would likely bring an Oscar nod. Even though it was a long shot, she put it in her valise with the other two scripts. Then she called Josh.

"Hey, Josh. Do you have a few minutes to meet with me? I've been looking over some of the screenplays you sent over, and there are a few that look really good."

"Sure! Want to say sixish? Seven? Eight?"

"Seven works for me," Tally said uneasily. "But don't you ever go home anymore?"

"Only to sleep."

Tally let that sink in. Something wasn't right. For Sadie's sake—and for Josh's—she wanted to find out what was going on. After their meeting, Tally would suggest that they grab a bite, maybe even have Sadie join them as well.

"I'll be there by seven."

When she got to ICA, most of the staff had already gone home, but a lone assistant was still manning the reception desk. Of course, the assistant recognized Tally and immediately punched a call button on the intercom. "Have a seat, Ms. Jones!" she said brightly. "I just rang Josh's assistant, Seth. He'll escort you in."

Tally grimaced. She'd had numerous opportunities to talk to Seth when he'd connected her with Josh by phone, and although he'd always been polite, there was a perpetual chill in his voice, despite her attempts to get him to warm up.

She busied herself with a copy of the latest *Vanity Fair*, which lay on the coffee table along with copies of *Variety, The Hollywood Reporter, People,* and the *Los Angeles Times*.

A full ten minutes passed, and still no Seth. The receptionist looked even more annoyed than Tally felt, and she buzzed him again. A moment later, someone else—another male assistant—came out into the reception area. The two assistants exchanged a few frenzied whispers, then the man walked off down the hallway.

Through the glass wall, Tally saw him enter the men's room. When he came out, he looked annoyed. Seth followed a second later. The last person to emerge was a scruffy guy whom Tally recognized immediately. He was an actor who had appeared in guest roles on numerous television shows. He was also a known drug dealer.

Ah, so that's it, Tally thought.

"Ms. Jones, great to see you again." Seth's smile was as placid as his tone. "Would you care to follow me back to Josh's office?"

Tally was shocked to discover that Josh was a lot thinner than the last time she'd seen him. He was also more anxious. He couldn't sit still and kept jumping up to stand in front of the floor-to-ceiling picture window that provided a million-dollar view of the Los Angeles skyline.

They spent the first half-hour discussing the pros and cons of the Scorsese and Spielberg scripts and the progress that had been made on each to identify a complete cast. During that time, Josh excused himself once to join Seth in the assistant's cubicle, located right outside the office. When he came back, he was even more wired than before.

Sadie was right; he was definitely using again. Tally resolved to set him straight at dinner by telling him how worried she and Sadie were for him. She'd even threaten to walk if she had to.

Tally had deliberately left Mac's project, *Tapestry*, for last. When she brought it up, Josh frowned. "Hmm. I'm guessing that for you, that project is a nonstarter."

"That's a shame. We both know I'd be perfect for it. Why hasn't Mac cast it yet, anyway?"

Josh fiddled with the pen in his hand. "That's a good question. Maybe he's waiting for Susie to be done with this season of *Dana Point*."

Tally couldn't believe her ears. "You're kidding, right? He's going to waste this role on her?"

Josh shook his head. "Look, Tally, I know you'd be ideal for the role. But let's face facts. Despite what you or I think of Susie's acting abilities, we don't control this project. Mac does." He lowered his voice. "And he told me that he doesn't want you in his life. Not even professionally."

His words landed on her chest like a boulder, and she felt as if she couldn't breathe.

Mac hates me that much, even after all this time? Well, then, Susie has officially won.

She took a beat to regain her composure, then said, "No harm in asking, right? How about calling Scorsese tomorrow and telling him I'd love his consideration if he still wants me." She shut her valise with a snap and stood up. "Care to join me at Nobu Malibu? Sadie can join us, too. There's something else I'd like to talk to you about."

Josh agreed, and they decided to take separate cars. After a quick call to Sadie, the plan was set. As he walked her to the elevator, Josh said he had forgotten something and had to go back to his desk. *He's getting his stash,* she thought. But she went along with it.

Tally got to the restaurant before him. Sadie was already there, and she was clearly upset. "I just got a call from the police! There's been an accident involving Josh, just down the road!"

"I'll drive," Tally said. Sadie grabbed her purse and followed her out.

The wreck was two miles from the restaurant on the Pacific Coast Highway. From what they could tell, it looked as if the car had spun out of control and hit a sixteen-wheeler head-on. The driver's side of Josh's car had been crushed.

The ambulance was already there, as were three police cars. Sadie ran up to the ambulance. What she saw stopped her in her tracks and brought her to her knees, screaming. They were zipping up a body bag.

Tally was at her side in a second, along with one of the policemen and a med tech. As her friend moaned in grief in the arms of the med tech, Tally grabbed the policeman's arm. "That was her husband. Can you tell me what happened?"

He frowned. "He was speeding when the officer over there came up behind him." He nodded at another cop. "The officer signaled for him to pull over, but instead, he hit the accelerator. We found an empty bag crammed in the ashtray. Maybe he had his eyes off the road for too long. Or he could have had an overdose. A toxicology report will show us for sure."

Tally thanked him, then crouched down beside Sadie and put her arm around her. "It's OK, I'm right here. Let me take you home."

The memorial service took place at Forest Lawn.

Because Josh represented many of Hollywood's elite, the service was well attended and star-studded. Sadie, with Mandy and Tally at her side, accepted the condolences of Josh's clients, partners, and staff.

Notably absent was Josh's assistant, Seth. Tally had reported to the police what she'd seen take place in ICA's offices less than two hours before Josh's death, and other office staffers verified her suspicions that both Seth and the actor might have been Josh's drug suppliers.

Tally noted that Richard and Elizabeth Carlton were at the service, as well as Mac and Susie.

"The nerve of her!" Mandy hissed to Tally behind Sadie's back when she spotted her friend's nemesis. "Look at what that bitch is wearing!" Susie had come in a low-cut red dress, with a wide-brimmed hat and big sunglasses more appropriate for salsa dancing than mourning.

Tally's makeup artist, Ben, had come, too. She was surprised to see him and gave him a warm hug. "I didn't realize you'd even known Josh."

"He was in my Cocaine Anonymous group. In fact, I was his sponsor once. But I had suspected he'd gone back to using when his assistant wouldn't put through any of my calls."

"You tried your best, and that's what counts," she said as she blinked away more tears.

Ben glanced around at the crowd. Something he saw made him smirk. "Well, well, well, isn't that interesting?"

Tally strained to see what had caught his attention. He was staring at Susie, who was conversing with Richard and Mac. She had her arm intertwined with Elizabeth's.

"Of course, they'd be here. Susie was one of Josh's clients, and Mac and Richard did numerous deals with him," Tally said.

"Oh, that doesn't surprise me," Ben said in a low voice. "It's Susie's audaciousness I'm referring to."

"I know! She looks like a hooker in that red getup. It's atrocious."

"No, not the outfit. I mean her coddling her lover's wife. Talk about gall!"

Tally looked at him sharply. "Ben, what are you saying?"

He leaned in closely. "I have it on the highest authority that Susie has been sleeping with Richard the Liver-hearted."

"You've got to be kidding me!" Tally whipped back around. "Why would she do that?"

Ben shrugged. "Why does Susie do anything? Because she can. Mac would never suspect it, and Richard always has at least one play pal on the lot at any given time. Not that I blame him. Look at Miss Elizabeth. Why, she's practically pickled."

Tally winced, even though she'd be the last to deny that Elizabeth was a lush. "Ben, are you absolutely sure that's true?"

"I got it from Garfield. The things that boy shouts out during sex would make a priest blush!" Ben's brow went so high it nearly pushed his hairpiece out of place. "Trust me, there's plenty of meat on that bone."

Tally stole a glance at Mac. She knew him well enough to be certain he had done what he could to make his marriage work, but it wasn't enough, and it never would be. He'd been lied to from the very beginning. Most important, he'd been lied to about Tally.

She was willing to forgive him. But Susie? *Never*.

It was payback time.

Chapter 31

TALLY WAS TOLD that Louis Cabrini was a go-to guy. People in Hollywood knew that if you wanted to cover up something really, really bad, he would take care of it, no sweat, and if you wanted something exposed, he'd find where all the corpses where buried.

In this case, more than one hot-blooded body had shown up in Susie's home in Coldwater Canyon. Apparently, she'd never rented it out, as she'd claimed to Mac when she moved into his Pacific Palisades spread.

Louis shook his head in wonder as he played the surveillance DVD for Tally in his dingy office. "That woman might as well install a revolving door in that bedroom of hers. Just take a look at this one twenty-four-hour period alone."

He clicked forward on the DVD. The time stamp showed that it had been taken three days after the funeral, on a Sunday. At the speed he was playing it, the sunlight moved rapidly across the house's tile roof, but the video was clear enough to make his point.

The first car to move through the gate and up the drive was a chauffeured Lincoln Town Car. Louis hit the play button just as Susie opened the door to greet Richard, who jumped out of the backseat with a bouquet of pink roses. While she embraced him, Susie said, "My favorite!" then nudged him inside.

Louis fast-forwarded the DVD a bit more. Richard had barely been gone two hours before another vehicle pulled up. This time, it was a jacked-up monster truck Tally recognized as Jared's. He fixed his hair in the mirror for a moment before Susie shouted for him to get his ass into the house, pronto. Whatever she had in mind apparently included the cat-o'-nine-tails she held in her hand. Tally shivered at the thought.

The third segment of the tape caught a well-known young female starlet going into Susie's place. Confused, Tally wondered what *she* was doing there.

Tally didn't recognize the car in the next segment—an old Jeep—but she certainly knew its driver when she saw him: Gabriel. Apparently, he'd had to sell his Porsche after he couldn't get any work. Susie opened the door nude, holding a honey bear, and the memory of the night Gabriel raped her came flooding back. Tally swallowed hard to keep down the bile.

"This has to be foolproof, Louis. I presume there's a way to prove she was meeting these people for sex, right?"

"What, are you kidding? That broad has a camera in every room! If she ain't in the porn industry, my guess is that she uses it for blackmail." He chuckled. "We tapped into her cameras wirelessly. Breaking her security code was a piece of cake. It's all here in living color, with Dolby sound to boot. I'll show you foolproof."

He clicked a button on the DVD remote, and a softly lit bedroom appeared on the TV screen. Susie was straddling Richard, who was moaning ecstatically. Louis fast forwarded the DVD until it came to Jared in the same room, down on all fours in front of Susie, who wore high-heeled boots and a mask. In the next interior shot, Tally saw Susie had one leg up on a chair. Her silk robe was wide open, allowing the starlet, who was now kneeling in front of her, to put her head in Susie's crotch. The ecstatic look on Susie's face left no doubt in either viewer's mind that Susie was enjoying herself immensely.

Oh my God, Tally thought. *When Susie dry-humped the strippers at Sadie's party, that was no act!*

Another few frames further into the video showed

Susie again, this time in her den. She was naked and bent over a chair as Gabriel poured something thick and gooey over her back.

There was more on the tape, but that was all she could stomach.

Again, a shiver went up Tally's spine. "I've seen enough. Thank you. The whole video covers, what, a full week?"

"Yep." Louis turned off the DVD player.

"Here's your cash." She handed him an envelope, and Louis popped the DVD out of the player and handed it to her. As she turned to leave, he said, "By the way, I loved you as that nun in *Cloistered*. Made me cry like a baby. It's been a pleasure doing business with you, Ms. Jones."

Chapter 32

THE DVD WAS waiting for Mac when he came into his office the next morning. The envelope was marked personal, and on it "SUSIE" was written in block letters.

Interesting, he thought. He'd never received so much as a love note from his wife. That just wasn't her style. At least, not since they'd said their I do's. Now he was getting a home movie from her?

He took the DVD to the closest monitor and put it on. It didn't take too long for the plot to sink in, particularly after his father drove up and kissed his wife as ardently as Mac had ever kissed her, and she responded in a way that she hadn't responded to him in quite a while. Mac went numb.

As the video segued to Jared, Mac was so angry he couldn't see straight. And by the time Gabriel was done with Susie, he was ice-cold.

He flipped off the monitor and buzzed his assistant. "Do me a favor, and send a dozen roses to my wife. Pink ones. The card should read, 'Because they're your favorites. See you tonight, eight sharp. Don't be late.' You don't have to sign it. Thanks, Carole."

He'd make sure it was a night Susie would never forget.

"You fucking bitch!" Jared yelled as he swung open the door to Susie's trailer. "How could you do this to me?"

Susie peeled back the cucumbers that covered her eyes. Her green mud face mask had just stiffened, so she felt safe enough to move her head to see what Jared was squawking about. As she sat up, he tossed the DVD case at her face. Well, there went the mask.

"Damn you, Jared! What the hell?"

"See for yourself." He snatched the DVD out of her hand and stalked over to her TV set.

At first, she didn't recognize the video's setting. When she did, she turned white under the mud pasted to her face. "Where the hell did you get this?" She grabbed him by the throat. "Where? Tell me!"

"I thought *you* left it for me. See? It has your name on it." He pointed to the envelope. "You're making out with that old asshole Richard Carlton? And Gabriel McNamara, that washed-up loser? How the hell could you do that to me?"

Susie shoved him out of the trailer and locked the door. She panicked at the thought that Richard might have a copy of this same DVD. Or, worse yet, Mac.

A knock on her door made her heart leap into her throat. "Jared, get the hell out of here!" she yelled.

It turned out to be one of the production assistants. "Delivery! Flowers!"

What the fuck? She opened the door to a bouquet of pink roses. She tore open the card. *Because they're your favorites. See you tonight, eight sharp. Don't be late.*

She breathed easier. So Richard didn't know. *Good. Now, if that idiot Jared does anything stupid . . .*

She called Burt Tillman and told him that Jared had finally lost it, that he was threatening her life. She demanded that he be escorted off the set—in fact, off the show—for good. Afterward, she was still so nervous that she walked onto the set without realizing her face was still covered with mud mask.

〰

On the drive out to her love shack, she made up her mind. She was tired of playing games. The sooner Richard left Elizabeth for her, the better. She was going to convince him of that tonight, and she planned on pulling out all the stops to make it happen. If Richard started yammering to her about his guilt again, she'd just remind him how Elizabeth had sucked him dry all these years. *Like one of her martini olives,* she thought. Then she'd remind him how Mac thought he was so much better than his father, now that he had two Oscars of his own. *You gave him everything, and what did he do? Left you,* she'd say. Richard would be furious with his wife and son and so entranced with her that he'd take that final step and commit to a divorce.

And not a moment too soon. Since Tally had left *Dana Point*, the ratings had plummeted, and it was only a matter of time before the show was canceled. But Richard could coerce any of the producers kowtowing to Royalton's studio boss to build a show around her. A *new* show. Maybe even a comedy.

She got home and began setting up for her life-changing rendezvous. By the time the doorbell rang, the candles were lit, soft music was playing, and rose petals—pink ones, from this morning—were strewn from the foyer to the bedroom. She had also changed into a sheer white negligee, which she wore with high heels.

She ran to the door and threw it open, only to find Mac.

"Surprise," he growled.

A cold trickle of dread went down her spine. *He knows . . . or does he?*

He looked around. Taking note of all the work she'd put into her little tryst, he let loose with a low, appreciative whistle, then followed the rose-petal trail that led into the bedroom. As he began unbuttoning his shirt, he looked back at her. "Aren't you coming?"

Susie was at a very interesting crossroads, and she knew it. The only way to keep the upper hand, she figured, was to grovel. So she decided she'd do it in the same manner in which she'd captivated him in the first place: with mind-blowing sex.

Slowly and seductively, she walked over to him. She took the zipper of his pants and pushed it down, leaning into him while she worked her magic. She tilted her head up to him, but he wouldn't kiss her. Instead, he took her by the hair and forced her onto her knees in front of him. She took the hint and put his cock into her mouth. As it grew, and even as he heard her gag, he thrust it deeply, again and again, until he exploded, then smiled as he watched her swallow.

Knowing she had pleased him, she shimmied onto the bed and spread her legs, anxious to get hers.

He laughed. "What, are you kidding? I got what

I wanted. Save that for Richard. Oh, and do me the favor and break the news to him that I'm on to both of you."

Then he walked out.

"Where are you going?" She shouted after him. "Oh, let me guess! You're going back to *her*."

That stopped him cold. "You know, that's not a bad idea."

Chapter 33

OK, SO NO BIG DEAL. Mac knew. He was bound to find out sooner or later. Granted, Susie had wanted it to come from her, but that wasn't going to stop her from dumping him for Richard.

She was in a terrible frame of mind, thanks to her messed-up personal life, and work wasn't making her feel any better. When she saw her script the next morning, she noted that her lines were tepid, void of any emotion. What did the writers think she was, an extra? She might as well have been part of the scenery.

I can't win an Emmy with lines like this. She fumed.

Then she remembered she was fucking the studio

head. *I don't have to say this drivel. I can say any-thing I want.*

"Quiet on the set," the director, Larry, called out. "OK . . . action!"

Spencer's line came first. *Blah, blah, blah,* thought Susie. When he paused for her response, she gave it: "No, Hank. I'll never agree to that! Not in a million years. I'll die first—"

"Cut!" Larry shook his head in exasperation. "Susie, what the hell are you reading? That's not any-where in the script. We're on page twenty-three, re-member?"

She stared right through him. She could tell it un-nerved him by the way he frowned.

Good, she thought. *Get ready for a fight.*

"OK, from the top, Spencer. And *action*!"

Spencer delivered his line again, and again, Susie responded just the way she wanted to.

"Cut!" Larry took a deep breath, then walked over to his star. He took her by the elbow and pulled her away from Spencer and the crew. "Look, Susie, I don't know what you're going for here, but whatever it is—"

"I'm going for authenticity, Larry. The lines I was given are pure garbage. You know it, I know it, and heaven knows the writers know it, too, because they are the ones who turned this crap out in the first place. Let me go with my gut here." Susie was determined to stand firm.

"This isn't the Groundlings, doll! It's a prime-time drama. And this scene is just one plot domino in a row of them, which is why your line has to be delivered in a certain way. Otherwise, the show doesn't make sense. You know that."

"I'll tell you what else I know, Larry. I know a bad script when I read one."

Larry closed his eyes and took another deep breath. "Susie, I'm not looking for an argument. I just need you to read the lines as they were written. Do I make myself clear?"

He presumed he had, because she went stone-faced and walked back over to her mark.

Larry nodded to the crew. "OK . . . and . . . *action.*"

For the third time, Susie read the line the way she wanted, completely ignoring Larry's direction and what was on her script. His next conversation with her wasn't as civil, and the brouhaha sent the assistant director scurrying off the set to call Burt Tillman. Another had already alerted a network suit to get down there fast, because it looked as if someone was going to get hurt.

Both the suit and Burt made it to the set at the same time.

"Susie, what the hell is going on?" Burt demanded.

She glared at him. "Larry doesn't get it. I don't like my lines, and I'm doing a different interpretation. And frankly, I don't know why you're here and not drinking your way into oblivion. Isn't it your happy hour?"

"I'm here because you're fighting with your director, and you're acting like a damn madwoman! Now, just read the lines as they're written."

"How *dare* you talk to me like that? Who the hell do you think you are?"

"The producer of this show. Now, if you know what's good for you—"

Before he could finish, Susie slapped him. Hard.

The cast and crew drew a collective gasp, and then there was silence.

Burt touched his raw cheek, straightened his back, and began walking off the set. As he passed Larry, he murmured something so low that only the director could hear it. Larry nodded silently in response.

Burt kept walking. As he exited the building, the network executive was right on his heels. The suit looked as if he'd seen a ghost.

As the door closed behind them, Larry called out, "That's a wrap," and everyone dispersed.

All alone on the set, Susie looked around, wondering what was going on. *That's it? But what about the scene?*

She headed back to her trailer. By the time she'd

washed off her makeup, her new agent, Dan Jacobs, was there, holding a sheaf of papers.

Susie smirked when she saw him. "Jeez, news travels fast. What do you want?"

"The network has a proposition for you, Susie. Obviously, the incident on the set isn't one that any of us would like to see hit the media."

She nodded grudgingly.

"Good. Glad you're in agreement. So here's the deal. If you sign this agreement and keep to its terms—in other words, keep your mouth shut about what will forever be known to those on the inside as 'the incident'—in return, you get a lump-sum check for a quarter of a million dollars."

Susie shrugged. Hell, if she'd known that she'd get that much, she would have smacked Burt years ago.

"However," Dan went on, "should you ever speak of the incident—to *anyone*—Burt will sue you into oblivion."

"Ha. Sure, OK. I can live with that." She grabbed the pen out of his hand and signed all four copies of the agreement with a flourish. Then Dan scampered out of there as quickly as he could without saying another word.

She'd just finished putting on her own clothes when there was another knock on the door. It was a PA with her script for the next day's scenes.

Susie had only one. In it, she was decapitated in a freak accident. That's when it hit her like a lightning bolt: *I'm being written off the show. No! This can't be happening.*

She dove for her cell phone. Dan's number was on speed dial, and he picked up on the second ring. "Hey, bring back those papers! I've rethought this deal."

"Sorry, Susie. I've already turned the contract over to Burt. The network was just couriered a copy, too—"

She slammed the cell shut.

This was the end. Her career was over, unless Richard would stand up and protect her. She had to see him—now.

She dialed his direct line, and when he picked up, she sobbed. "Richard, it's your Pink Precious. I need you so badly. I can't take it any longer! It's Mac—he *beat* me. I can't believe I'm still alive. I'm asking him for a divorce. I was so upset that I messed up really badly on the set today, and now Burt is writing me off the show! Well, at least I'll finally be all yours, Richard. Can we meet? Yes! Our usual place, in an hour."

Chapter 34

MAC HAD TO see Tally. He needed to tell her he realized he'd fucked up royally, that he had been wrong about them, that he'd been a fool to listen to Susie all along, that he loved her and knew now that he couldn't live without her.

He tried to call her, but she had changed her number, and he didn't know who her agent was now that Josh was gone. Then it hit him: Sadie would know how to reach Tally.

He dialed Sadie's cell-phone number. When she picked up, he apologized for disturbing her during this time of grief and asked her how she was doing. As he listened to her talk, her pain was obvious in her voice, despite her attempt to sound normal. Having lost someone he loved very much, too, his heart broke for her.

When it seemed as if she'd talked through all of her anguish, he casually asked, "So, how's Tally doing these days?"

Sadie was so silent that Mac thought she'd hung up on him. Finally, she said, "It's about damn time you got around to asking that question, Mac Carlton."

He exhaled. "Well, at least you didn't slam the phone down, then call her and have a good laugh at my expense."

"I don't think Tally would laugh, Mac. To her, what you two had was never a joke."

That was all Mac needed to hear before begging for her phone number. His next call was to the love of his life.

It was dusk when he got to her place. As he drove through the gate, the memories of their times there flooded back to him. His heart was beating quickly, and he had to clear his throat a few times to remind himself that he could still talk.

Tally greeted him at the door dressed simply in jeans and a white V-neck T-shirt, and he noticed she was barefoot. She looked even younger than he remembered her. Certainly younger than her age. *She's the most beautiful woman I've ever seen,* he marveled.

She took his hand and drew him into the living room. It was just as he remembered it, cozy and inviting. Then they walked out to the pool. He was surprised to discover she'd made dinner for them, just as she'd done on their first date in Paris, and the food was laid out on a table between the chaise longues, where he'd asked her to marry him.

He hated the thought that he'd wasted the last three years without her and silently vowed to spend the rest of his life making up for that.

She looked at him with tears in her eyes, and he yearned to kiss her. But he knew better. Instead, he said, "It's nice of you to see me, Tally. I'm hoping you'll consider working with me—"

She put a finger to his lips, silencing him. "First things first."

She kissed him for a long time, then pulled back.

"Why did you leave me?" she asked quietly.

He thought back through the fog and pain of the past three years, during which he'd buried his hurt with work and with down-and-dirty sex with Susie. And yet all that time, he'd fantasized about the woman standing before him.

He supposed that by doing all those things, he was somehow punishing Tally. And at that moment, he remembered why he had wanted to punish her. She wanted to know why? OK, he'd tell her.

"Gabriel."

Her eyes grew wide with surprise. "What about Gabriel?"

I can't believe she's acting so surprised, he thought.

"There was a video of him—with you." He closed his eyes wearily. He was done playing games.

"Seriously, Mac, I don't know what you're talking about."

"Tally, come on, already, fess up! The video must have been taken a couple of nights before our wedding day. It was shot in your trailer. You were in a bathrobe, and he went inside with you—"

"Gabriel, with me? Oh! I remember now. He came over, desperate to see me, right after work one day. He was so hopped up on pills, he fell on top of me. I took him inside so he could sit down, and I went to get him some water. By the time I got back with it, he'd taken off."

She's lying, Mac thought. *What a mistake this was!* "Oh, yeah? That's not what I saw."

"What did you see? When?"

"Susie had a video of you."

Hearing her rival's name, Tally raised an eyebrow. "Oh, yeah? Tell me more."

"I've already told you. It was you and Gabriel." He

choked out the words. "You were straddling him. Just what a guy wants to see before he's getting married!" Mac ran his hands through his hair. The thought of her with her ex just before their wedding day still made his blood boil.

Now Tally was angry, too. "I swear to you, that never happened. Are you sure it wasn't Susie with a wig? Considering she had something to do with you seeing it in the first place, I'm guessing that would be more likely."

"The video only showed you from behind." He sat down slowly. "My God, are you suggesting that she faked that whole thing?"

"Knowing Susie, I'd say that's a likely possibility." She looked him right in the eye. "But I'm guessing the video she sent me on the night we were supposed to get married—of the two of you screwing—was the real thing. In fact, I still have it."

His silence spoke volumes.

"Thought so." Tears glistened in her eyes. "Even after seeing that, I hoped you'd come to your senses, that you'd come to see me so we could talk. I believed you would—until I saw your wedding photos in *People*." She looked down into the pool. "After that, I was so upset I had a miscarriage."

"You were pregnant—with our baby?" It felt as though his heart had just been pierced.

"Yes. I was going to tell you on our honeymoon."

When he took her in his arms, she didn't fight him. Instead, she leaned into him, as if speaking of their lost child had finally released her from the pain she'd felt over the past three years.

His eyes misted over with tears. "I'm an idiot. That conniving bitch played me like a stupid schoolboy. If I'd had any sense, I would have confronted you first."

"She was betting that your ego would stop you. And she was right." Tally stroked his face with her finger. "Mac, listen. What's done is done. We can't change the past."

"You're right. And we've got the rest of our lives to make up for it." He cradled her face in his hands. "In fact, I'm serving her with divorce papers tomorrow. Wait. Did you send me the video of Susie?"

She smiled. "You know what they say, all's fair in love and war. When I heard what she was doing to you . . . I'm sorry, but I couldn't let her get away with that."

He sighed. "Don't apologize. You did me a favor."

"Does Richard know yet?" Tally was almost afraid to ask.

"I told Susie she'd better inform him. My guess is that she's doing that right now."

"Mac, why do you think she went after him?"

"In her tiny brain, he's the next rung up on the

power ladder." He frowned. "My poor mother. I guess
I should get over there now, to console her when she
finds out. Which she inevitably will." He stood up.
"Tally, I know my mother treated you miserably, and
there is no excuse for her doing so. Still, if you could
stomach it, I'd appreciate your company on the ride
out there."

"If you need me, I'm there."

Mac believed that more than anything he'd ever
heard in his life.

Chapter 35

NEVER FIGURED YOU to be a submissive. Are you sure about this?" Rosanna, whom Susie had not seen since the night they'd framed Burt Tillman at the Chateau Marmont, was poised to strike Susie across the back with a leather whip. Usually, Rosanna was on the receiving end, and needless to say, she was worried about what Susie might do in retaliation.

Susie was getting exasperated. She needed to make good on her lie to Richard about Mac beating her. "It's not brain surgery, you dumb bitch! Look, Richard will be here any minute. A couple of stripes across the back is what we're going for here. Now, just do it!"

Rosanna slapped the whip across Susie's back and

winced as Susie cried out in pain. She did it harder the second time, and Susie yelped again.

Then again.

"Damn it!" Susie was sobbing. "Enough already!"

Rosanna got in one more quick strike before she untied Susie, who was moaning in agony. She grabbed Susie's cash and was almost out the door when the vase Susie threw at her missed her head by six inches. To Rosanna, it was worth it.

It took three very long hours to convince Richard that tonight was finally the night to leave Elizabeth. Or, as Susie put it, to "take me away from Mac, that brute son of yours."

The tears helped, as did the hot sex. But it was the lashes on her back that put him over the top.

"My son is a monster!" Richard fumed. "Of course, you have to divorce him."

"And you'll divorce Elizabeth?" Susie let loose with a new stream of crocodile tears.

Richard's shrunken shoulders caved in even more. "Yes, Susie."

She smiled angelically. "I'll ride over to Pasadena with you. I think we should break the news to her together, don't you?"

She couldn't wait to see the look on that old witch's

face when he told her. She also wanted to be there to make sure he didn't back out on their agreement.

Mac and Tally were already in the living room with Elizabeth when Richard and Susie pulled up.

When Susie saw Mac, she grabbed hold of Richard's arm. "Please make sure he doesn't get anywhere near me," she whispered melodramatically.

Mac looked at her as if she were crazy. "I wouldn't touch you with a ten-foot pole. In fact, considering all of your extracurricular activities, I guess now is as good a time as any to ask when was the last time you were checked for STDs."

"There—you see what I mean, Richard? Do you see what I have to put up with?" The tears started to fall again.

"I'm warning you, son. Stay away from my future wife."

"So, what Mac says is true. You're here to ask me for a divorce?" Elizabeth cut in. She was holding the ever-present Baccarat tumbler filled with gin. Her voice trembled, but she looked Richard in the eye.

Richard seemed to deflate a little. "I'm sorry, Elizabeth, but yes."

"I see." Elizabeth slowly sank onto the settee. "And when do you plan on marrying?"

Susie smiled triumphantly. "As soon as possible. After my divorce with Mac is final."

"Well, yes, dear. Otherwise, you're a bigamist." Elizabeth looked at her with disdain. "From what I've gathered already, you are a lot of things—bitch, trollop, whore—but not that. At least, not yet."

"Mother, my attorney files tomorrow. From what I gather here, Susie isn't contesting my action." Mac gave Richard a pitying look. "Are you sure this is what you want?"

Richard hesitated just long enough for Susie to nudge him from behind. "Yes. I haven't loved your mother for years."

"You've had enough whores to prove that to me, Richard." Elizabeth's eyes swept over her husband angrily. "Oh, don't look so shocked. Of course, I know about all the women! I still have friends at the studio, too, you know. If this is what you want, there's nothing I can do to stop you."

Tally suddenly remembered what Ben had said about Garfield. *He must have been her gossip conduit,* Tally thought.

Elizabeth raised her head high. "When I learned of this betrayal—of both me and Mac—I asked my attorneys to file for legal separation this morning."

"Good," Richard said, clearly relieved. "Then it's settled. I'll have my attorneys get in touch with yours.

I've no doubt you'll want this tomb of a house, and I'm willing to give it to you."

"That is truly generous of you, Richard. Then again, you wouldn't be able to afford it anyway, since you'll be out of a job."

Richard frowned. "I don't know what you're talking about."

It was Elizabeth's turn to smile. "Then I presume you've forgotten that I own the largest share of Royalton stock."

Richard did a double take. "But—but that stock was only put in your name for tax purposes! Besides, it's not enough to swing a vote with the board of directors to have me ousted."

"No," said Mac, "but with her block, my block, and my producing partner Elena Hahn's block, we've pretty much got it covered. In fact, I just got off the phone with Elena. She's having her attorney draw up a proxy for me to cast any way I see fit."

Richard turned white.

"The fact that you've sunk so low as to take your own son's wife— I'm sorry, Richard, but that is unforgivable." Elizabeth shuddered. "Your things are being packed and placed in the limo as we speak. Your driver will take you wherever you want to go, but he has been informed that you'll no longer need his services after tonight."

Susie couldn't believe her ears. "Wait, you'll no longer be head of the studio?" She looked from Richard to Elizabeth to Mac and finally to Tally. "*You!* You sent that video around, didn't you? Why, I ought to—"

She lunged for Tally, but the younger actress was too quick for her. Tally delivered an uppercut under her chin, and Susie collapsed on the floor.

Standing over her, Elizabeth scrutinized Susie's jaw. "Ah, well. She was due for a chin job, anyway. Up until now, I was too polite to say anything, but those saggy jowls are so unattractive in profile."

Chapter 36

IN TALLY'S OPINION, the best time of day in the honeymoon suite at the George V was right at daybreak. Particularly after a vigorous night of lovemaking.

As they stood at the terrace's French doors, taking in the most beautiful sight in Paris—the sun's first rays striking the Eiffel Tower—Tally leaned into Mac and breathed a contented sigh.

"Happy?" he murmured in her ear.

As if he needed to ask. "The only thing that would make this any more perfect is if we could stay just one more week." She nuzzled his neck lovingly. "But I guess there's no chance of that, Mr. Big Shot Studio Head."

"I'd quit in a second if that's what you wanted." He sounded as if he meant it.

She smiled but shook her head. "It's the job of a lifetime, and you're just the man for it. You've been in training for this role all your life."

"Here's hoping I live up to our stockholders' expectations as well."

"Mac, your track record speaks for itself. Don't you read *Variety*? According to the trades, you're the best thing that's ever happened to Royalton Studios—and it was a long time coming, too."

"I think what really made them happy is that Royalton now has a first-look deal with Oscar-winning actress Tally Jones's new production company."

Tally laughed. "You can thank my new manager for that! Who knew Sadie Fletcher was such a brilliant negotiator?"

"We all did. Even Josh, God rest his soul, knew she was the real power behind that throne."

He pulled her down onto the bed with him and kissed her. After lying side-by-side silently for a moment, Tally sat up, sensing something was bothering him.

"Mac, is something wrong?"

He sighed. "I was just thinking about my father."

Tally lifted his chin so that they'd be eye-to-eye. "Your father made some pretty bad mistakes, most of them at his stockholders' expense. With you running the studio, you can right his wrongs, and he'll make money whenever you do. He still owns a lot of stock in Royalton. And as for Susie, well, getting dumped by her was the best thing that could have happened to him."

"Yeah, I guess you're right." He looked at his watch. "Well, we should get going. How gauche would it be to be late to your own wedding?"

"Yo, juicy Susie, are you ready for your close-ups?" By that, Susie's new producer, Jerry Conover of Dandy Candy Productions, meant the ones that were to zoom in on the various male organs she was currently handling.

After word got out that she'd slapped Burt Tillman, everyone who was anyone came to the same obvious conclusion: *Susie Sheppard will never work in this town again.*

Well, she was proving them wrong. Sort of.

Granted, Chatsworth wasn't on the most celebrated side of the Hollywood Hills, but it, too, was dedicated to the film industry, and Dandy Candy had welcomed her with open arms. Now that Taylor Made was going mainstream—thanks to her new manager, Sadie Fletcher—the studio needed some classy new talent, and it eagerly embraced Los Angeles's most celebrated fallen star.

This was only a temporary setback—at least, that was what she kept telling herself. Besides, the way Susie saw it, being in porn had its upside. Already, in three very short months, she had racked up more movies than most actresses her age made in a lifetime. And considering her age—her *real* age—that was saying a lot.

While her novice gangbang movies were popular, they weren't as much fun for her as the girl-on-girl scenes. But if Susie had learned one thing, it was that timing was everything, and she was willing to bide her time and work her way into the coveted dominatrix roles. And when she did, once again, Susie Sheppard would be on top.

ACKNOWLEDGMENTS

SO MANY PEOPLE have helped me along the way on this journey and have helped me realize my hopes and dreams. I want to thank all of you from the bottom of my heart! Harry Hamlin, my amazing supportive husband. My mom and dad, who are the wind beneath my wings. Delilah and Amelia, who teach me daily how to love. I'm so proud to be your mom. My sister, Nancy; my niece, Tracy; and Dorie, thank you for your love and support.

Thank you to all of the Team Rinna members who have made me who I am. Without them, who knows what I'd be! My PMK-BNC publicists, Jill Fritzo and Meghan Prophet, who guide me through the publicity machine in such a graceful, fun way! To my attorney, William Sobel, who is the best there is and who has my back at all times, thank you, Bill!

The glam squad, Faye Woods and Adam Christopher—love you! Thank you Dan Strone for introducing me to the world of books. Jennifer Bergstrom, who took a chance on me, and then took another chance on me, thank you for believing!! My editor, Emily Westlake, thank you for your guidance and patience. Jonathan Swaden for checking all the things off my list, thank you for getting me here. UTA and CAA, thank you. Steven Grossman, to all the magic to come! You rock!!! And last, but certainly not least, Miss Josie Brown, without whom this book would not be possible!!! You rock, girl!